ILLUMINATING
ANGELS
&
DEMONS

ILLUMINATING ANGELS & DEMONS

The Unauthorized Guide to the Facts
Behind Dan Brown's Bestselling Novel

SIMON COX

Sterling Publishing Co., Inc.
New York

Library of Congress Cataloging-in-Publication Data Available

10 9 8 7 6 5 4 3 2 1

Published in 2005 by Sterling Publishing Co., Inc.
387 Park Avenue South, New York, NY 10016

First published in Great Britain in 2004 by
Michael O'Mara Books Ltd

Copyright © 2004 Simon Cox

Distributed in Canada by Sterling Publishing
c/o Canadian Manda Group, 165 Dufferin Street
Toronto, Ontario, Canada M6K 3H6

Sterling ISBN 1-4027-2456-X

Designed and typeset by Design 23

Printed and bound in the United States of America by
Quebecor World, Martinsburg, WV

Fiat lux

From the opening chapter of the Latin Bible,
"Let there be light"

CONTENTS

Introduction

For many, *Angels & Demons* will be the second Robert Langdon adventure they have read, after the international bestselling novel *The Da Vinci Code*. However, what they may not realize is that *Angels & Demons* is actually the first of Dan Brown's novels to feature Robert Langdon. The leading character in these books, Langdon is a compelling hero, part Sherlock Holmes and part Indiana Jones, and his impressive erudition and quiet courage have no doubt contributed greatly to the popularity of both novels. Of course, a number of other elements have contributed to the success of *Angels & Demons*, such as the use of symbolism, shady secret societies, dark church history, clues and riddles to solve, Roman history, and much else. It's a combination Brown used to great effect in the follow-up book, *The Da Vinci Code*—substituting Paris, London, and Roslin for Rome—and one that will no doubt prove equally as successful in future Robert Langdon adventures.

Angels & Demons is a thought-provoking book, not least because of its underlying theme of Church versus science. Dan Brown uses the "big bang" creation theory, together with its attendant concept of antimatter, as a major plot device within the story, juxtaposing this with traditional Church values and beliefs. This centuries-old conflict between men of science and men of religion is as relevant today as it ever was, and Brown uses it as a springboard to explore a number of related themes in the book.

In this he has benefited from the recent development of a more widespread interest in the science of our cosmic origins. Once the exclusive preserve of white-coated experts, in the last couple of decades scientists such as Carl Sagan and Stephen Hawking have broken down the walls of this sacred enclave to let us all peer in. The general public now has an appreciation of some of these very deep and complicated issues, a number of which are discussed within the pages of *Angels & Demons*. Dan Brown has helped to propel the popularization of this subject by condensing and simplifying scientific theories in such a way as to make them more understandable to the general reader. Indeed, after finishing the book many readers will find themselves debating issues and questions that may never before have arisen in their conversation.

As in *The Da Vinci Code*, Dan Brown uses the traditions and machinations of the Catholic Church for the backdrop to his narrative. In recent times, and due to the publication of these two novels, Brown has found himself challenged by members of the clergy and lay people alike over his perceived anti-Church stance. Yet it would be unfair to say Brown's motive for writing these books is merely to grind his literary axe against Catholicism or religion in general. More likely, he is simply using 2,000 years of bloody but immensely interesting history as the perfect canvas on which to paint his fantastic stories. Indeed, it could be argued that the Church has failed to seize upon a brilliant opportunity when faced with these novels. After all, regardless of how many millions of books Brown sells, his literary longevity will be as a drop in the ocean when compared to that of the Bible. By opening up the places mentioned in Brown's novels and welcoming visitors with open arms, the Church might not only bring in extra income, but would also have an opportunity to refute and put right some of the errors that it criticizes in Brown's writing. Sadly, my experience when undertaking research for this book shows that the Church has actively taken the opposite approach. One example of this is the decision to rope off the Chigi Chapel in the Church of Santa Maria del Popolo, a key location in *Angels & Demons*, for no apparent reason other than to stop "Dan Brown tourists" from investigating this fascinating corner of Rome.

Brown's inclusion of the so-called "Father of the Baroque," Gian Lorenzo Bernini, in *Angels & Demons* was an inspired decision. This remarkable sculptor, painter and architect has left an indelible mark on the face of modern-day Rome. Bernini is everywhere: his spirit is ever-present, and his legacy within the fabric of Roman society remains all-pervasive. Whether Bernini was ever a member of an anti-Church secret society, intent on world domination and the end of all governments and religion, is another matter entirely—and, as stated in the entry for Bernini in the following pages, evidence for this is very scant and actually points to the contrary conclusion. Nonetheless, Dan Brown's choice of Bernini for the role of master Illuminatus is to be applauded, bringing, as it will, tens of thousands of people to the work of this virtuoso.

The shadowy presence of the secret society known as the Priory of Sion is felt throughout *The Da Vinci Code*; in *Angels & Demons*, the Illuminati adopts the same role. A five-minute trawl through a search engine on the Internet will bring up literally thousands of sites dedicated to discussions about the Illuminati. Ninety-nine per cent of these websites simply regurgitate secondary-source material and fantastical stories that have no basis whatsoever in reality. Indeed, the net result of conspiracy theorists going into overdrive and cases of paranoia spiraling out of control has been that real research and genuine facts have been buried amid the mass of wild and baseless speculation. This isn't to say that such secret societies don't exist, or that some form of world government or domination is not on the agenda—but these arguments may be for another book entirely. The idea that Big Brother is out to get you and that a secret cabal of the elite and the educated are plotting the damnation of us all is not a new one. Since time began, men have plotted and others have suspected. Groups of like-minded individuals will always band together, forming societies, clubs, and gangs, with agendas that rarely emerge beyond the halls of their meeting places. This fact is part of the human condition.

Yet again Dan Brown has, I believe, rendered us all a great

service. His use of certain themes has encouraged many people to discover more about subjects such as the arts, history, the Church and Christianity, secret societies, and cabals and fraternities. His books serve as a window onto many intriguing and enlightening subjects, and indeed act as a gateway into areas of research and knowledge that many would have passed by had they not picked up a Dan Brown novel.

Robert Langdon is the questioner and inquisitive soul that we all want to be; his insights and perceptions help us to challenge received wisdom. In doing so, we can all become ultimately "illuminated."

Simon Cox
London, October 2004

Ambigrams

Although you won't find this word in a modern dictionary, according to the website www.ambigram.com the definition of the word "ambigram" is: "Ambigram *n.*,—a word or words that can be read in more than one way or from more than a single vantage point, such as both right side up and upside down (from the Latin: *ambi* meaning 'both' and *gram* meaning 'letter')."

One of the finest contemporary proponents of this art form is a certain John Langdon. It was Langdon who was responsible for the beautiful ambigrams within the pages of *Angels & Demons* and who, it could be surmised, may have lent his surname to the central character and hero of the book. The four individual designs for "Illuminati"—earth, air, fire, and water—are in themselves impressive, and with the "Illuminati diamond," or combination of the latter four words, Langdon has achieved a masterpiece.

Ambigrams fall into three common types. The rotation type of ambigram is probably the commonest. These ambigrams are rotated 180 degrees and can be read the same upside down as they are right side up, a classic example being MOW. The reflection type of ambigram employs a form of mirror-image symmetry: these words can be read normally when reflected in a mirror—a good example would be TOOT. However, some reflections can be read as different words when rotated—such as MOM, which becomes WOW. Chains are styles of ambigrams that depend on being linked to the words around them, sometimes forming an interlinking pattern. These chains can be made up of either rotation or reflection ambigrams.

It would seem that ambigrams have been around for quite some time, and there are many common ambigram symbols and shapes that most people would recognize. Dan Brown mentions some of these himself within the novel— the Jewish symbol of the Star of David, the yin-yang symbol, and the swastika being notable examples.

See also: Illuminati; Langdon, Robert.

Antimatter

A difficult concept to understand, "antimatter" is a term used to describe certain types of subatomic particle studied in quantum physics. At a basic level, all matter is made up of atoms, which in turn are made up of electrons, protons, neutrons, and many even smaller particles, all of which are known as subatomic particles. During the 1950s and 1960s, it was proved that every subatomic particle has a corresponding "antiparticle," which has the same mass as a given particle but opposite electric or magnetic properties. Collectively, these antiparticles are known as "antimatter."

In 1930, the scientist Paul Dirac proposed a radical new approach to the question of the motion of electrons in magnetic fields. His theory was the first to make correct use of Einstein's theory of special relativity in this context. Dirac put forward the idea that quantum theory, which had been used to describe the behavior of electrons, actually required there to be another type of particle, with the same mass as the electron, but with a positive instead of a negative charge. These particles were christened "positrons," and thus the theory of antimatter was born.

According to Dirac's predictions, all particles must have an antimatter equivalent, with the mass of any antiparticle identical to that of the corresponding particle. These antiparticles also display signs of reverse charges—for example, a positively charged proton will have a negatively charged antimatter proton as its variant. The existence of antimatter has since become a central pillar in the discipline of quantum theory.

Modern theories of particle physics and quantum theory propose that matter and antimatter were found in equal quantities in the earliest stages of the universe's creation after the "big bang." However, this poses something of a puzzle today, as antimatter is actually highly unstable and does not occur naturally on earth. Any antimatter created in a laboratory is immediately destroyed

the moment it meets up with matching matter particl
resulting annihilation creates pure energy. This en
then carried by further particles that can, in turn, dec
yet more particles. So, where are the equal amounts of
antimatter that should exist, along with all the matter we
can observe in the universe? Data currently being collected
by NASA suggest that clouds of antimatter may be evident
in the galactic center, but that matter dominates the
universe as a whole. The antimatter theory leaves us with
more questions than answers, but it may yet hold the key to
proving once and for all how the universe was created.

In *Angels & Demons*, the use of antimatter as a potential
doomsday explosive device forms one of the central themes
of the story. Is it possible to harness the energy within
antimatter in this way? The answer is yes . . . or possibly . . .
or at least not at the moment, anyway. The collision and
annihilation that result when antimatter and matter meet do
indeed create the potential for a huge release of uncapped
energy, but this would be incredibly difficult not only to
capture and isolate from matter, but also to control. NASA
researchers have postulated that such an energy release
could be harnessed as part of an antimatter/matter
propulsion system that could be developed for deep
interstellar travel some time in the future. Scientists at such
institutions as CERN (Conseil Européen pour la Recherche
Nucléaire) in Switzerland have been working with particle
accelerators to try to create antimatter that can be
harnessed and controlled. At CERN they actually managed
to create an "antiatom"—a nucleus with one antiproton
plus an antielectron—in 2002, which was an astonishing
achievement. In fact, it seems that it isn't so much the
complex levels of science and technology involved in
antimatter production that are problematic, but more the
financial costs of such work.

The potential consequences of the production of
antimatter have permeated their way into modern culture

and the media. In 1950, Isaac Asimov postulated in *I, Robot*—since made into a blockbuster movie starring Will Smith—that a robot could be endowed with the equivalent of a brain via an element of antimatter that would mimic human neurons. Many more books and science-fiction TV shows and films have also used antimatter as either a device for evil destruction, or as a propulsion system (as in *Star Trek*).

See also: Big Bang Theory; CERN; Einstein, Albert.

Apocrypha

At one point in the novel, Camerlengo Ventresca visits the Papal Vault, which contains all the information and objects that the Church believed were too "dangerous" for the public to know about. Included in the list of objects were the fourteen books of the Apocrypha. In fact, the Apocrypha contains many more than fourteen books if one takes into account both Old Testament and New Testament Apocrypha.

The term "apocrypha" comes from the Greek for "hidden," and is used to denote certain books and texts that are not part of the approved biblical canon. The Apocrypha fall into two groups: the Deuterocanonical Apocrypha (texts that are or had once been included in some versions of the Bible, but are generally omitted nowadays for textual or doctrinal reasons), and other Apocrypha (texts that have never been included in the recognized canon, but are nevertheless useful in understanding historical, legendary, or mythological aspects of the Bible). Among many other works, the latter includes a collection known as *The Forgotten Books of Eden*, which consists of The First Book of Adam and Eve, The

Second Book of Adam and Eve, The Book of the Secrets of Enoch, The Psalms of Solomon, The Odes of Solomon, The Letter of Aristeas, The Fourth Book of Maccabees, The Story of Ahikar, The Testaments of the Twelve Patriarchs, The Testament of Reuben, The Testament of Simeon, The Testament of Levi, The Testament of Judah, The Testament of Issachar, The Testament of Zebulun, The Testament of Dan, The Testament of Naphtali, The Testament of Gad, The Testament of Asher, The Testament of Joseph, and The Testament of Benjamin.

The New Testament Apocrypha includes The Infancy Gospel of James (supposedly written by James the Just, the brother of Jesus), The Arabic Gospel of the Infancy, The Gospel According to the Hebrews, The Gospel According to the Egyptians, The Gospel of St Peter, The Gospel of St Philip, The Gospel of St Thomas, The Gospel of St Bartholomew, The Gospel of the Twelve Apostles, The Report of Pilate to the Emperor, The Gospel of Nicodemus, and The Narrative of Joseph of Arimathea, as well as the The Acts of St Peter, The Acts of St John, The Acts of St Andrew, The Acts and Martyrdom of St Matthew, The Acts of St Thomas, The Acts of St Bartholomew, The Acts of Saints Peter and Paul, The Acts of St Paul, The Acts of Paul and Thecla, The Acts of St Philip, The Acts of St Matthew, The Acts of Simon and Jude, and The Acts of St Barnabas. This is by no means an exhaustive list, as there are many other Apocryphal texts including letters, teachings, and apocalyptic literature.

Dan Brown revisits the Apocrypha in his subsequent bestselling novel, *The Da Vinci Code*. The plot of this book is based on the premise that the Church suppressed information contained in the Apocrypha about the role that Mary Magdalene played historically in the life of Jesus. The Gospel of Thomas and The Gospel of Mary Magdalene are the primary Apocryphal sources that he uses for this theory.

The Apocrypha has long been a fascinating source for scholars of alternative history, intent on gaining real insight into the mysteries of the biblical age and the origins of Christianity. Though the Apocrypha is now widely available to interested parties, the Vatican's Secret Archives still house material of a sensitive and controversial nature, thus fueling the interest of alternative historians worldwide.

See also: Vatican, The.

Armageddon

Robert Langdon and the Camerlengo are high above Vatican City when the antimatter is released. The crowds below witness a blinding flash and a thunderous explosion; the shockwave knocks the spectators off their feet. Dan Brown likens this to Armageddon.

The term "Armageddon" has become synonymous with an apocalyptic event leading to the end of the world, as mentioned in the Book of Revelation 16:16: "And they assembled the kings [of earth] at the place which is called in Hebrew Armageddon." Armageddon is therefore designated to be the place where a large force will gather for the great day of battle between God and the kings of the earth; a battle between the forces of good and the forces of evil. At this time the world will witness lightning and thunder, a violent earthquake and the ruination of all cities. Islands and mountains will vanish and great hailstones will fall to the earth. This will be followed by the final judgment of all souls and the salvation of the just.

The Book of Revelation has proven to be an irresistible draw for groups who believe that the contents of the prophecy will manifest themselves as real events, and that we are actually in these so-called "end times" right now. Many secret societies and pseudo-religious groups find great symbolic significance within the pages of Revelation.

The word "Armageddon" is thought to derive from the Hebrew *har-Megiddon* or "mount of Megiddo," probably a reference to the fact that the city of Megiddo was situated on a large hill in what is now northern Israel. Holding a strategic position on a pass through the Carmel mountain range, Megiddo controlled the important trade routes between Mesopotamia, the Levant, and Egypt. Accordingly, it has been the site of many important conflicts, notably the battle fought by the Egyptian pharaoh Thutmose III in 1468 BC, who was eventually able to re-establish Egyptian authority in the region only after a seven-month siege of the city. During the First World War, British, Dominion and Empire forces defeated the Turkish army at Megiddo, thereby ultimately transferring control of Palestine to the British.

See also: Vatican, The.

Bede, St

On their way towards the Pantheon to try to prevent the first murder of a cardinal, Robert Langdon and Vittoria Vetra discuss the meaning of the phrase "demon's hole" and why this could possibly be used to describe the circular opening in the Pantheon's roof. Langdon comments that the English monk known as the Venerable Bede had written about the fact that in an attempt to escape the newly consecrated church, demons had made the hole in the building's roof.

Although Langdon states that Bede wrote in the sixth century AD, he actually lived in the seventh and eighth centuries—he was in fact born in 672. He is known as an outstanding author and scholar who wrote on all subjects, though principally theology and history. One of his most famous works is the five-volume *Historia Ecclesiastics Gentis Anglorum* ("Ecclesiastical History of the English"), detailing the history of the English people from the Roman occupation until 731. Within the fifth volume, Bede added some autobiographical details about his life, informing us that at the age of seven he entered the Benedictine monastery of St Peter at Wearmouth, in the north of England, in order to train as a monk. A few years later, he moved to another Benedictine monastery, St Paul's in Jarrow, where he remained until his death on May 25, 735.

The Venerable Bede appears to have been well read and fully conversant with such classical writers as Pliny the Younger and Ovid. In addition to being fluent in Latin—as was expected of a monk—Bede could also read Greek and some Hebrew. Among his many works are *The Life and Miracles of St Cuthbert, Bishop of Lindisfarne*, two works on chronology, various scientific works (Bede described the world as being round like a ball, rather than "round like a shield"), essays on grammar, commentaries on the Old and New Testaments, and an Anglo-Saxon translation of St John's Gospel, which he completed on his deathbed. His writings provide us with a hint of his character, that of a kind, sympathetic, and caring person whose piety is unmistakable. On his death, his possessions were distributed to the other monks, though his worldly belongings consisted only of some incense, peppercorns, and a few handkerchiefs. In 836 the Catholic Church declared Bede venerable, and in 1899 he was canonized, becoming St Bede the Venerable.

Dan Brown's reference to the Venerable Bede and the "demon's hole" may be a misinterpretation of a section of Bede's *Ecclesiastical History of the English*, Book II, Chapter IV. In this chapter, Bede relates a story of how Mellitus, the

Bishop of London, went to Rome to confer with Pope Boniface about the affairs of the English Church. As part of this chapter, Bede mentions that Pope Boniface "obtained for the Church of Christ from the Emperor Phocas the gift of the temple at Rome called by the ancients Pantheon, as representing all the gods; wherein he, having purified it from all defilement, dedicated a church to the holy Mother of God, and to all Christ's martyrs, to the end that, the company of devils being expelled, the blessed company of the saints might have therein a perpetual memorial."

In other words, the Venerable Bede merely relates a story of how the Pantheon became a Christian church, with no mention of devils leaving the newly ordained church via the hole in the roof.

See also: Pantheon, The.

Bernini, Gian Lorenzo

As a master sculptor, painter and architect responsible for many of the finest works of art in Rome, Bernini provides the locations that lead Robert Langdon and Vittoria Vetra around the city on their search for the missing cardinals.

Born in Naples, Italy, in 1598, Gian Lorenzo Bernini was the son of the celebrated sculptor Pietro Bernini, who moved to Rome in 1606, taking his talented son with him. They worked together on sites such as the Pauline Chapel in the Church of Santa Maria Maggiore and the Villa Borghese. Cardinal Scipione Borghese, who had been a protector of the artist Peter Paul Rubens, became an important patron of the young Bernini, and as the nephew of Pope Paul V he introduced him to the world of papal patronage. During this time Bernini worked on life-sized sculptures of classical figures such as Aeneas, Anchises, Pluto, and Persephone, his work displaying technical virtuosity and an understanding of the art of antiquity. He had restored ancient sculptures for the Borghese family and he later stated that as a youth he sketched ancient works "as if they were an oracle." When Pope Paul V died, Bernini designed the catafalque for the body (a temporary raised platform on which the deceased lies in state), which resulted in one of the first examples of his combined sculptural and architectural talents.

During the short papacy of Gregory XV, Bernini was made a *cavaliere* (knight) and a member of the Accademia di San Luca—honors bestowed on him for merit; he is depicted in portraits wearing the cross of insignia (a mark of office) and carrying the sword of a knight. It was with the appointment of Maffeo Barberini as Pope Urban VIII, however, that Bernini's future became assured. Barberini was renowned for his support of poets and he had himself written verses in Greek and Latin—Rubens and Bernini illustrated some editions of his work. The newly elected pope received Bernini at an audience and is said to have announced, "Great is your good fortune to see Maffeo Barberini Pope, but much greater is ours that Cavalier Bernini lives during our papacy." With an endorsement like that it is perhaps not surprising that Bernini's mother said that her son acted "almost as if he were master of the world."

Commissions flooded in and Bernini widened his activities to include painting, architecture, stage design, and writing plays. He remodeled the Church of Santa Bibiana in Rome and his architectural duties extended to the Palazzo Barberini, a building that boasted a new architectural style, the Baroque. One of Bernini's most significant works was the baldachin, a symbolic structure erected over the supposed tomb of St Peter in the basilica then being remodeled at the Vatican. This monumental piece was built between 1624 and 1633, stands at 85 feet (26m) high, and was cast from 927 tonnes of metal taken from the roof of the Pantheon across town. Bernini also designed the four piers that support the basilica's dome, the *cattedra* that houses the papal throne, and eventually the tomb of Urban VIII and the artist's later patron, Alexander VII. Bernini's influence also extends outside to St Peter's Square, where he designed the colonnade with its 284 columns and statues of 140 saints. Around the obelisk in the square is an elliptical set of markers to the points of the compass. It is one of these, *West Ponente*, that in *Angels & Demons* represents the element of air, as its other name—*Respiro di Dio*, or the "Breath of God"—suggests.

There was, however, one less successful element to Bernini's work on St Peter's. He began to erect bell towers over the façade, but their weight started to crack the building, and they had to be pulled down in 1646, temporarily diminishing Bernini's reputation. An interruption in papal commissions allowed him to produce the Cornaro Chapel in the Church of Santa Maria della Vittoria, which includes the sculpture *The Ecstasy of St Teresa*. The angel in the piece holds a spear tipped with fire, which Robert Langdon recognizes as a vital clue to the location of the next murder. In *Angels & Demons*, Bernini's *Fountain of the Four Rivers* in the Piazza Navona represents the element of water in the final location of Langdon's search; the fountain was a work that impressed Pope Innocent X and ensured that Bernini's studio was kept busy.

Popes came and went, but the role of Bernini as a founder of the Baroque era, and main architect of St Peter's, continued. On the day Pope Alexander VII ascended the papal throne, Bernini was summoned to see the new Holy Father to discuss plans for the completion of the basilica; Alexander VII (formerly Fabio Chigi) also turned to Bernini for his family chapel. The Chigi Chapel in the Church of Santa Maria del Popolo already contained works by Raphael; to these were added sculptures by Bernini, including one depicting the Old Testament prophet Habakkuk—who foretold the destruction of the Judeans—and an angel. The chapel also contains the cover to an ossuary for collective burials, referred to in *Angels & Demons* as the "demon's hole." In the novel, this proves to be the location of the first element—earth—and the site of the first murder of a cardinal.

In 1665 Bernini made a trip to Paris after repeated invitations from Louis XIV, of whom he sculpted a bust that set a standard for heroic royal portraits. As a renowned artist, Bernini received a splendid welcome in France, and the writer Paul Fréart de Chantelou kept a diary of his visit. He reports that Bernini acknowledged "he attended to his work with great care, but that there must also be something else, suggesting that it was the grace of God to which he attributed everything." This contemporary account is at odds with any suggestion that Bernini may have been an opponent of the Church, or a member of a dissident organization such as the Illuminati. Bernini also submitted plans for the Louvre, but these were abandoned after his departure from France, possibly due to the jealousy of French architects. After six months away from the projects that he referred to as his "children," Bernini returned to Rome. Among his later works were the angels nicknamed "Bernini's Breezy Maniacs," sited on the Ponte Sant' Angelo (which helped to guide Langdon in his quest to find the Hassassin in *Angels & Demons*), and the Altieri Chapel in San Francesco a Ripa, Rome.

Financial hardship in Rome forced Pope Clement X to make cuts in spending, and during the early 1670s the city authorities published a resolution against "Cav. Bernini the instigator of popes to useless expenses in such calamitous times." They recommended that he "make his living with statues" and from that time he received no more architectural commissions.

By the time Bernini died in 1680, at the age of 81, he had served eight popes and designed some of Rome's most splendid tombs and monuments. By contrast, his own burial was a modest affair: he was laid to rest in a joint family tomb within the Church of Santa Maria Maggiore in Rome, the site of some of his early works.

Speculation is rife, particularly on the Internet, as to Bernini's association with certain secret societies, including the Illuminati. It has proved impossible to find any contemporary or historical evidence to back up these suggestions. That said, Bernini evidently designed the ellipse of St Peter's Square as a nod to Copernicus's heliocentric (sun-oriented) view of the solar system, a theory at odds with Church doctrine at that time. Though it seems clear that Bernini, being a man of science and art in equal measure, was indeed "illuminated" (or enlightened) in this sense, his fascination with such subjects would certainly not have stretched to his creating a "Path of Illumination" for supposed Illuminati initiates.

He had great interest in the symbolism of Egyptian obelisks, for instance, placing one in St Peter's Square; from the basilica, the axis of the square follows an eastern direction, toward the rising sun, signifying the resurrection of Christ.

See also: Castel Sant'Angelo; Chigi Chapel; Ecstasy of St Teresa, The; Fountain of the Four Rivers; Habakkuk and the Angel; Illuminati; Obelisks; St Peter's Basilica; Santa Maria della Vittoria; Santa Maria del Popolo; West Ponente.

Big Bang Theory

Robert Langdon is familiar with the big bang theory before he arrives at the CERN laboratory, as he tells Vittoria Vetra and Maximilian Kohler. They have to explain it to him in more detail, however, in order for him to understand the significance of the antimatter that has been stolen. It is also an opportunity for them to discuss the contribution made by science and religion to the development of theories of creation.

The "big bang" could easily be a metaphor for the clash between the Church and science over the question of these theories about the universe's origins. Yet what most people don't realize is that this most radical of astronomical and scientific theories was actually first postulated by a Belgian priest called Georges Lemaître, in 1927.

Lemaître's theory asserts that the universe has its origins with the explosion—the big bang—of the first primeval atom, a kind of cosmic egg, consisting of subatomic particles and radiation. American scientist Edwin Hubble also became convinced that the universe had formed in such a manner, after he made observations that suggested everything within the universe is continually expanding, and discovered that a galaxy's speed of movement is proportional to its distance from the observer.

The big bang theory has now become the dominant scientific explanation of the origins of the universe. According to the core theory, the universe was created some 10–20 billion years ago from the cosmic explosion of the first atom, with matter hurled in all directions and vast amounts of energy being unleashed. The scientists Arno Penzias and Robert Wilson are credited with further confirmation of the theory when they found evidence of a cosmic background radiation left over from the actual big bang explosion itself—a discovery that earned them the Nobel Prize for Physics in 1978.

There are several problems with this model, however.

According to the theory, because of the initial big bang it was predicted that the distribution of matter throughout the universe would be uniform. This argument was named the Cosmological Principle, and postulated that the distribution of galaxies within the universe should be predictably uniform in shape and number. Lately, though, scientific research has shown that there are ribbons of superclusters of galaxies, hundreds of millions of light years long and millions of light years thick, and that there are also vast voids within space, some of which are as much as 300 million light years across, where we would expect to find galaxies.

As recently as 1989, two scientists from the Harvard-Smithsonian Center for Astrophysics, Margaret Geller and John Huchra, published their map of the universe, revealing what they called the "Great Wall," a massive area of galaxies 200 million light years across and 700 million light years long. These clusters stretch across about one-fourth the diameter of the universe, roughly about 7 billion light years. The problem is that under the conventional big bang theory, these clusters and voids would have needed some 150 billion years to form, based on the speed of movement they are showing—much longer than the conventional big bang theory allows for.

The concept of the big bang has caused much consternation within religious circles, with Creationists dismissing the theory out of hand. Some religious organizations welcomed the idea, though, arguing that it still relied upon the creation of the primeval atom, or cosmic egg, and that its subsequent explosion and expansion can only be explained by a guiding principle—in other words, God. In *Angels & Demons*, Dan Brown has incorporated this dichotomy within the fabric of the novel by means of the character Leonardo Vetra. This CERN scientist, working on the development of antimatter, is also a Catholic priest.

So what was there before the primeval atom? And what caused it to go "bang" when it did? God only knows.

See also: Antimatter; CERN.

Bilderberg Group

The year 2004 marks the fiftieth anniversary of this secretive, and some would say sinister, group. Robert Langdon includes the Bilderberg Group as a possible financier for the Illuminati. The organization has been a focus of conspiracy theorists the world over for a number of years now. But what exactly is the Bilderberg Group? Who are its members? And why do they meet up at all?

The group's origins lie in the ruins of postwar Europe. Ostensibly seen as a way of bringing leading political and business figures together from both the USA and Europe, the first Bilderberg meeting was held in 1954 at the Bilderberg Hotel in Oosterbeek, the Netherlands—hence the name of the organization.

The most influential figure in the early days of the group was Prince Bernhard of the Netherlands, who organized and chaired the first three-day meeting. However, the Bilderberg Group seems to have been the brainchild of one Joseph Retinger, who started life as a Polish émigré. Along with Frenchman Jean Monet, Retinger would go on to become one of the prime instigators behind the foundation of a European Movement (now the European Union) after a speech that he gave in 1946. To conspiracy theorists and Eurosceptics, Joseph Retinger was both a modern-day *éminence grise* and a one-worlder, determined to help build a new world order after the Second World War.

Operating without political portfolio or office, Joseph Retinger is one of those mysterious figures from history who seem to have had an influence and power base disproportionate to their standing. Retinger could list as friends and close confidants such luminaries as Winston Churchill, David Astor (the British newspaper tycoon), Averell Harriman (the business tycoon and US politician), General Sikorski (the Polish government leader in exile during the Second World War), and the aforementioned Prince Bernhard. Indeed, it was Prince Bernhard who admitted in the foreword to a biography of Retinger that the latter "was, in point of fact, the prime mover" of the Bilderberg Group.

Prince Bernhard was himself a colorful character. Ostensibly the founder and titular head of the Bilderberg Group, he also founded the World Wildlife Fund in 1961, and enjoyed a large degree of political influence both in Europe and at the United Nations. Bernhard was German-born, the son of Prince Bernhard von Lippe; it was via his marriage to Princess Juliana of the Netherlands that he assumed the title Prince of the Netherlands. Once a member of the German Luftwaffe—and thought by some to have also been a member of the Reiter SS Corps—Bernhard fled to England with the rest of his family when the Germans invaded the Netherlands at the beginning of the Second World War; he was viewed with much suspicion by the Allied command. However, after the war Bernhard was rehabilitated into the political and business spheres of the new and emerging Europe by American and British political insiders, joining the boards of a number of big corporations, businesses, and foundations.

It seems that in 1952, Joseph Retinger approached Prince Bernhard with the idea of forming a group of influential political and business heads from Europe and the USA, who could meet in secret and discuss the future of transatlantic relations. The Bilderberg Group was born and quickly established itself as one of the most influential and secretive groups in the world, along with the Council on Foreign Relations and the Trilateral Commission—two non-governmental organizations (NGOs) which are reputedly think tanks, but whose sway over domestic and foreign policy in the West seems disproportionate to their status.

Among the attendees at the first Bilderberg Group meeting in 1954 were: David Rockefeller, head of the global banking group (and later a chairman of the Council on Foreign Relations); Dean Rusk, who would go on to become a US Secretary of State; C. D. Jackson, the head of the Time Inc. organization; Denis Healey of the British Labour Party; and General Walter Bedell Smith, a former head of the OSS (the Office of Strategic Services—a precursor of the CIA).

Today's Bilderberg Group meetings are still shrouded in the aura of mystery that surrounded those very first meetings. No press releases are ever produced at the meetings and the group have no visible website or other major public-relations presence. The Bilderberg Group have been accused of everything from causing the war in the Balkans to the latest developments in Iraq, all accusations that they naturally refute. The British economist and writer Will Hutton, who had been invited to one Bilderberg meeting, famously wrote of the group that "The consensus established is the backdrop against which policy is made worldwide," fueling the conspiracy theories further. However, Denis—now Lord—Healey challenges such claims: "There's absolutely nothing in it. We never sought to reach a consensus on the big issues at Bilderberg. It's simply a place for discussion."

Modern-day Bilderberg delegates include US Senator John Edwards, statesman Henry Kissinger, President of the World Bank James Wolfensohn, John Browne (chief executive of the petroleum firm BP), and former US president Bill Clinton.

At the meetings, no resolutions are proposed, no votes taken, and no policy statements issued. In short, Bilderberg is a flexible and informal international leadership forum in which different viewpoints can be expressed and mutual understanding enhanced. Two-thirds of the delegates come from Europe and the remainder from the USA and Canada. Those in attendace are solely invited for their knowledge, experience, standing, and relevance to the topics on the agenda. All participants attend Bilderberg in a private and wholly unofficial capacity.

All members agree not to give interviews to the press during the meeting. In contacts with the media after a conference it is an established rule that no attribution should be made to individual participants of what was discussed during the meeting. There are no press conferences.

The Bilderberg Group has attracted criticism and accusations of conspiratorial machinations from both the extreme right wing and the left, with right-wingers accusing the group of being a bunch of Zionist plotters and the left certain that the group are planning a global business and political policy.

It is hard to know the truth about the Bilderberg Group. The secretive nature of the organization has certainly inspired a rabid interest among the more way-out conspiracy theorists. Perhaps the group really is just a business and political think tank, set up to help US–European relations. The truth itself probably lies somewhere in the middle, but one thing's for sure: the Bilderbergers aren't telling.

See also: Freemasonry; Illuminati; Knights Templar; Langdon, Robert.

Boniface VIII, Pope

In *Angels & Demons*, it emerges that the Pope has been murdered, an idea that seems shocking both to most of the characters in the novel and to ourselves as readers, though Robert Langdon recalls that there has been speculation on previous occasions when the papacy has changed hands in suspicious circumstances. Boniface VIII is a particularly notable example—not only for his own death, as described below, but also for the suggestion that he may have instigated the murder of Celestine V to achieve his position.

Born Benedict Caetano, at Anagni, Italy, in around 1235, Pope Boniface VIII trained as a lawyer and had risen to the rank of cardinal by 1294, when he advised Pope Celestine V on the matter of his resignation from the papacy. On Christmas Eve, later that same year, Boniface was himself elected head of the Catholic Church. The retired Pope Celestine was subsequently held in the castle of Fumone and died soon afterward—his death was widely believed to be suspicious at the time, and has been investigated recently, as described in a separate entry. Boniface was quite the opposite of his predecessor in character, being both arrogant and combative, but he was a great patron of artists. He commissioned several statues of himself and numerous paintings, especially by Giotto.

Boniface opposed Philip IV of France over the taxation of the clergy without papal consent. Philip was subsequently excommunicated, an act that damaged the cohesion of the French Church. Many of the clergy, perhaps for their own safety, supported the king. Boniface issued the papal bull (decree) *Unam Sanctam*, reaffirming the superiority of the Church over temporal authority—a supremacy that devout Catholics believe stems from powers inherited from Christ. His message was that every human being is subject to the Roman pontiff. Boniface appointed the ambitious and unprincipled Albert I, a Habsburg, as

Holy Roman Emperor in return for an oath of absolute obedience to the papacy, thereby further alienating the French king.

During an invasion of Italy, Boniface fell into French hands for two days, and it is likely that he was mistreated. He never fully recovered from his capture and died on October 11, 1303, shortly after returning to Rome; by this time he was probably in his eighties. Although Boniface almost certainly died of natural causes, most likely an infected abscess, the circumstances were suspicious enough to give rise to allegations of murder.

Among Boniface's achievements were his defense of the authority of the Church and the publication of the *Liber Sextus*, a book of canon law. The fact that his predecessor, Celestine V, was still alive at the time of his election gave his enemies, particularly the powerful Colonna family, the opportunity to question the validity of his papacy. It is interesting to note, however, that much of Europe was shocked at Boniface's ill treatment by Philip's friends and allies. The Swiss Bishop of Sion predicted that the French king and his progeny would lose the crown as a result, a prophecy that was fulfilled within 25 years.

See also: Celestine V, Pope.

Camerlengo

The Cardinal Camerlengo of the Sacred College of Cardinals is an official who holds a special position after the death of a pope. It is his duty to verify that the Pope is dead by calling his baptismal name three times, and traditionally by striking the pontiff's forehead with a ceremonial hammer. On the assumption that he receives no reply, he removes the Fisherman's ring from the third finger on the right hand of the late pope, and orders the papal seal on the ring to be broken. The death is then announced, and the process of conclave begins to select the successor to the papal throne. In *Angels & Demons*, the camerlengo not only carries out these duties, but he also plays an important role in the subsequent events of the novel.

In addition to arranging the burial of the deceased pope, and the election of his successor, the camerlengo has other duties. The day-to-day running of the Church is managed by the camerlengo alongside three other officials—the Cardinal Bishop, Cardinal Priest, and Cardinal Deacon. Collectively, the four are known as the "Particular Congregation."

Once the election of a candidate has been confirmed, and the position has been accepted by the new pope, the camerlengo places the Fisherman's ring on the pontiff's finger. The appointee is then introduced to the world by the camerlengo with the words, *"Habemus papem"*—"We have a pope."

Other Church officials also carry the title "camerlengo" (which means 'chamberlain' in Italian), but fulfill different duties. The Camerlengo of the College of Cardinals is responsible for the financial administration of the college and officiates at the funerals of deceased cardinals. The Camerlengo of the Roman Clergy is elected by the parish priests and canons of Rome and has an honorary place in processions; he is also the arbiter of who takes precedence (e.g. who walks in front of whom) in ceremonial functions.

See also: Papal Conclave.

Castel Sant'Angelo

This imposing building on the banks of the River Tiber may not actually be the Illuminati lair suggested in *Angels & Demons*, but it has had a checkered past, and was certainly used as a place of imprisonment.

Built originally by the Roman Emperor Hadrian as a mausoleum, work started in AD 123 and was completed sixteen years later, after Hadrian's death. The cylindrical tower is more than 200 feet (61m) in diameter and 65 feet (19.8m) high, and was originally faced with marble and decorated with statues, including a colossal statue of Hadrian. A bridge was constructed across the river—now called the Ponte Sant'Angelo—and the best view of the castle is probably from this bridge.

The thick walls withstood the attacks on Rome by Goths in 537—though besieged, the city was not conquered. The former tomb thus began a new life as a fortification and has been modified several times, most notably in 1277, when it was connected to the Vatican by a covered passageway, known as the *passetto*. In *Angels & Demons*, the *passetto* provides the route by which the cardinals are kidnapped, and is also the route Robert Langdon and Vittoria Vetra use to flee the Castel Sant'Angelo after their encounter with the Hassassin.

During an outbreak of the plague in Rome in 590, Pope Gregory the Great saw a vision of the archangel St Michael on top of the building warding off the pestilence, and it was subsequently renamed Castel Sant'Angelo. Throughout history the popes have retreated to this fortress, most notably in 1537 when Clement VII fled to the castle during the sacking of Rome, and remained there for several months. Subsequent popes had the apartments decorated and enhanced to ensure a comfortable stay if they ever had to retire there. Less fortunate were the 200 people killed when the original bridge collapsed in 1450 under the weight of pilgrims to the city. As a strong fortress it proved suitable not only as a papal refuge, but also as a place of containment for enemies of the Church. Two notable detainees were the philosopher Giordano Bruni and the sculptor Benvenuto Cellini.

A restored Ponte Sant'Angelo was decorated with a series of statues of angels, dubbed "Bernini's Breezy Maniacs," because of the way their clothing appears to be whipped by the wind. Most of the angels were actually created by Bernini's pupils—though according to his designs—and erected in 1688, after his death. The master carved two angels himself, one holding a sign bearing the letters INRI ("Jesus of Nazareth, King of the Jews"—the Latin inscription placed on the cross at Christ's crucifixion), and another holding the crown of thorns, which were greatly admired by Pope Clement IX. When the angels were installed on the bridge, it was decided that copies should be made to protect the originals from the elements; having been replaced by the copies, the original statues now stand in the Church of Sant'Andrea delle Fratte, in Rome.

The action at Castel Sant'Angelo in *Angels & Demons* takes place after 11 p.m., which perhaps explains why the characters appear to have the building to themselves. During the day the site is thronged with tourists visiting the papal apartments, dungeons, and the Museum of Weapons and Armor that is housed in some of the old guard rooms.

The Castel Sant'Angelo also appears in Puccini's opera *Tosca*. The griefstricken heroine plunges to her death from the castle's terrace into the River Tiber below.

See also: Bernini, Gian Lorenzo; Rome.

Celestine V, Pope

In *Angels & Demons*, after it is discovered that the Pope has been murdered, Robert Langdon reflects on the historical precedent of Pope Celestine V, who was rumored to have been murdered at the hands of his successor, Boniface VIII (who himself was to die in similarly mysterious circumstances). Langdon remembers the story that a recent X-ray of Celestine's remains apparently revealed a hole in his skull consistent with the wound a large nail would cause if driven into the head.

Pietro da Morrone was about 85 years old when he was elected to the papacy on July 5, 1294, more than two years after the death of his predecessor. Born an Italian peasant, he became a Benedictine monk but subsequently chose to lead the life of a hermit in the Abruzzi Mountains near Sulmona. Other hermits joined him around the year 1260.

It was much to Morrone's consternation and astonishment that he was called to fill the office of Holy Father and become Pope Celestine V. A devout man of God, he was reluctant to jeopardize his own prospects of salvation by the earthly distractions of such power, but was persuaded that the holy position was too important to turn down. He was not capable of the organizational role he was required to fulfill, however, and relied too heavily on Franciscans, who were ascetics like himself, and also King Charles II of Naples. Celestine V agreed to take up residence in Naples, and attempted unsuccessfully to broker peace between Naples and the Kingdom of Aragon, and between England and France. The tasks were beyond him, though, and he resigned on December 13, 1294.

His decision gave rise to a theological conundrum: 'Is a pope's resignation lawful?' Could his successor—Boniface VIII—be considered the legitimate pope? After much debate, it was decided that he could, but rather than allowing Celestine V to return to his hermitage, as he desired, the papal authorities placed him under supervision.

After an escape bid he was imprisoned in Fumone Castle near Anagni, on Boniface VIII's orders, where he died on May 19, 1296.

Dante's *Inferno* places Celestine V at Hell's gate for his cowardice in relinquishing his papal duties. Surprisingly, seventeen years later he was canonized by Pope Clement V.

And what of the rumor about a hole in Celestine V's skull, mentioned in *Angels & Demons?* There does indeed seem to be some truth in this. An article from the Associated Press news agency, dated August 23, 1998, reads thus:

> After centuries of speculation that the thirteenth-century pope Celestine V was murdered, an Italian monk now claims he has proof, saying there is evidence that someone drove a nail into the pontiff's skull.
>
> Several Italian dailies quoted the Rev. Quirino Salomone as saying a CT scan performed on Celestine's mummified remains 10 years ago showed a half-inch hole in the left temple.
>
> None of the accounts explained who ordered the test or why the results were not revealed for a decade. Salomone said he is writing a book based on "scientific and photographic material" backing his thesis.
>
> "I hope to clarify for good the mystery of the pope's death," he said.
>
> According to the monk, the CT scan was performed in the spring of 1988 shortly after the remains were returned following their theft from L'Aquila's cathedral, 70 miles [112.7km] northeast of Rome.

See also: Boniface VIII, Pope; Heparin.

CERN

The Conseil Européen pour la Recherche Nucléaire—better known by the acronym CERN—is the world's largest particle-physics research facility and Europe's major center for nuclear research. It is based in Switzerland and is a vast complex, involving some twenty nations who contribute to its financial upkeep and add to the 3,000 people who work there. The organization's convention was ratified in 1954 by 12 member states. Its director general until 2008 is Dr R. Aymar.

CERN is a strange and unique place. To physicists it is the equivalent of Mecca. It attracts the most brilliant physicists from all over the world to work on purely academic questions about the basic structure of matter and the origin of the universe. To most laymen, its output is incomprehensible except in the most general terms, but at the same time its research raises questions of deep religious significance.

Rarely does CERN produce anything of any commercial value. The one outstanding exception is the World Wide Web. CERN needed something to enable the processing of information between scientists from different universities and research labs across the world. In response, Tim Berners-Lee, a British scientist working at CERN in late 1990, conceived of the idea of the Web and came up with many of the protocols and conventions that still underpin the Internet today.

Over the last 50 years, CERN has built increasingly large and more powerful "particle accelerators." The latest is something called the LHC (Large Hadron Collider) Ring, which is currently due to go online in 2007. This massive machine will be the world's largest structure of its type. Using a ring of magnets buried deep in a tunnel, some 16.5 miles (26.5km) in length, the LHC will accelerate protons (fundamental constituents of all matter) simultaneously in opposite directions around the ring, to virtually the speed of light, and then enable them to collide head-on. These collisions release phenomenal amounts of energy, which can result in the production of matter and antimatter. Scientists are hopeful that the LHC Ring will enable them to answer a number of questions—such as the issue of whether antimatter is the perfect reflection of matter, and whether there are extra dimensions of space and time— which have been predicted by models inspired by so-called "string" theory. The data generated by the project will be in the region of 12–14 petabytes—roughly the equivalent of 20 million CD-ROMS—and all this will require analysis by some 70,000 of today's fastest microprocessors found within the humble PC. This data management will be overseen by something called the LHC Computing Grid Project, which will be deploying a worldwide computational grid service, integrating the computing power of various scientific centers around the world.

The current member states of CERN are: Austria, Belgium, Bulgaria, the Czech Republic, Denmark, Finland, France, Germany, Greece, Hungary, Italy, the Netherlands, Norway, Poland, Portugal, the Slovak Republic, Spain, Sweden, Switzerland, and the United Kingdom.

Interestingly, on Wednesday September 29, 2004, a ceremony took place at CERN to "Illuminate the LHC Ring." Either somebody at CERN has a great sense of humor, or that title is a potential clue as to who really controls the organization . . .

See also: Antimatter; Big Bang Theory.

Chigi Chapel

This chapel, part of the Santa Maria del Popolo church in Rome, contains a concentration of work by some of the greatest artists who have ever lived in the city. In *Angels & Demons* it is associated with the element of earth, as the church becomes the site of the first of a series of grisly murders of the four abducted cardinals.

In 1513, a wealthy Italian banker named Agostino Chigi commissioned Raphael to design tombs for himself and his brother Sigismondo. The tombs have an unusual pyramidal structure over them, and it is likely that this design was copied from earlier Roman tombs, as the province of Egypt had a great influence on ancient Rome. Raphael also designed the mosaics in the vault, while the altarpiece is by Sebastiano del Piombo. Agostino, Sigismondo, and Raphael all died before the chapel was completed, however, and so by 1526 work on the project ceased.

The chapel was rejuvenated when a great-nephew of Agostino, Fabio Chigi, became Pope Alexander VII. He arranged for Gian Lorenzo Bernini to alter the façade of the church and make additions to the family chapel. One of the sculptures that was added is a marble statue depicting the Old Testament prophet Habakkuk and an angel. The pair have been caught at the moment the angel lifts Habakkuk by the hair and carries him to Babylon to bring food to Daniel in the lions' den. A statue of Daniel is also present in another niche of the chapel.

On the floor of the chapel a mosaic in the shape of a skeleton covers the entrance to the family burial place. It is one of a number of such entrances in the floor of the church, and marks a place where the remains of several family members could be interred together. This is the ossuary annex or "demon's hole" referred to in the story, and matches the clue provided in the verse Robert Langdon and Vittoria Vetra are using as their guide. At the end of his life, Bernini himself was buried in a similar structure in the family grave at the Church of Santa Maria Maggiore in Rome.

The Chigi family coat of arms is displayed many times in the chapel and elsewhere in the church. The insignia of six mountains and a star appears on the mosaic floor of the Chigi Chapel and on the domed roof. In the novel, the coat of arms is described as a pyramid and a star, which is correct only in that the six mountains are depicted stacked up and therefore form a pyramidal shape.

See also: Bernini, Gian Lorenzo; Habakkuk and the Angel; Illuminati; Obelisks; Pyramids; Raphael.

Colosseum and Roman Forum

Flying over Rome, Robert Langdon and Vittoria Vetra are impressed by the city's sights, including the vast Colosseum and the ruins of the once great Roman Forum.

Originally called the Flavian Amphitheatre, work on the Colosseum began in AD 72 by the Roman Emperor Vespasian, was continued by Titus, and completed by Domitian in AD 80. It was in use for some 450 years as a place of entertainment for the citizens of Rome until 523, when the last games were staged there. Subsequent earthquakes and the expense of staging the contests meant that the Colosseum was gradually abandoned; many of its building stones were looted and it eventually fell into ruin.

The games for which the Colosseum became famous consisted of gladiatorial combats, hunts, re-enactments of land and sea battles, and animal combats such as bulls fighting bears or lions fighting tigers, as well as criminals and prisoners of war fighting each other or animals. The inaugural games of AD 80 lasted a staggering 100 days and resulted in the slaughter of 9,000 animals.

Built mainly from travertine stone, the Colosseum is a huge elliptical building, encircling a 6-acre (2.4ha) arena. The façade is 158 feet (48.2m) high, separated into four levels, of which the bottom three contain 80 arches on each level. The interior is separated by half columns: Doric in style on the first level, Ionic on the second, and Corinthian on the third. The fourth level contains windows on every second panel, and originally the undecorated panels were hung with bronze shields. The arena was large enough to accommodate 60,000 people seated and another 10,000 standing. It had 80 entrances, which were numbered and so designed that the entire stadium could be emptied within a matter of minutes. The seats were allocated to the heads of households on a strict rotation basis. Each allocation was free of charge and the holder was supplied with a wooden ticket that informed them of the entrance number, row, aisle and seat number.

The arena floor was made of wood, and covered with canvas and sand. There were removable sections within the floor to allow animals to be raised up directly into the arena by the use of lift mechanisms. Below the arena floor were a number of passageways and rooms that contained cages for the wild animals, sections for the gladiators and prisoners, stores, and tools.

An awning served to protect the spectators from the sun and was held in place by 240 wooden beams. On one occasion, after the crowd apparently displeased the Emperor Nero, he ordered the awning to be rolled back and forbade the crowd to leave their seats, which led to the death of a number of people from heatstroke.

The Roman Forum is situated next to the Colosseum, separated only by the fourth-century Arch of Constantine. The Forum is now in ruins, but was once the political and religious focal point of the Roman Empire, consisting of temples, markets, and other important buildings, including the Regia and Curia. The Regia, or House of the Kings, dates back to the seventh century BC, during the time of Numa, the second King of Rome. It contained a shrine to Mars and was visited by Roman generals before they went to war to ensure a favorable outcome. In 45 BC, Julius Caesar incurred the wrath of Rome by moving his residence to the Regia, a move that many considered to be high-handed and arrogant. He also built the Curia, a large square building where the Senate met. The Curia was restored in the twentieth century, when reproduction bronze doors were mounted, and a new ceiling was installed, the original of which would have been gilded. Inside there are three tiers on each side where 300 senators could be seated on their folding chairs. The speaker's platform can be seen in the center of the red, yellow, green, and white marble floor.

There are many temples in the Roman Forum, although in most cases little more than a few broken columns now remain. These include: the Temple of Julius Caesar, built on the spot where the Roman emperor was cremated; the Temple of Romulus, built in AD 309; the Temple of Antonius and Faustina, which is probably the best preserved of the temples; the Temple of Vesta; the Temple of Castor and Pollux, dating to 484 BC; the Temple of Saturn, which housed the treasury and mint; the Temple of Concordia Augusta; and the Temple of Vespasian and Titus, which still has three columns remaining.

Three basilicas, or churches, can also be seen in the Forum, but once again, little of these remain other than the ground plans and broken columns. These are the Basilica Emilia, dating to the second century BC, which contained the law courts and money-changers; the Basilica Julia, built in 50 BC by Julius Caesar; and the Basilica of Maxentius.

The House of the Vestal Virgins is also located in the Forum, though now it consists of only a few low walls. It was built by Nero in the second century AD to house the priestesses who kept alight the sacred flame to the goddess Vesta. The priestesses had to remain virgins for the thirty years they served the goddess. If they failed to do so they were buried alive and the guilty man was flogged to death.

Three arches complete the monuments of the Roman Forum: the Arch of Septimus Severus, from the third century AD; the Arch of Augustus; and the Arch of Titus.

Over time the Roman Forum gradually fell into disuse, but its decline was hastened by Constans II, the Emperor of the Eastern Empire, who, on a visit to Rome in 667, ordered the removal of all the metal cramps from the buildings, commanding that the metal be melted down for armor to help him fight the war against the encroachment of Islam. Unfortunately, the cramps were vital protection for the buildings against earthquakes, and by the ninth century most of the buildings had collapsed and lay in ruins.

See also: Pantheon, The; Rome.

Copernicus, Nicolaus

Robert Langdon and Maximilian Kohler mention the name of Copernicus when they are discussing scientists who have been persecuted or murdered at the behest of the Church. In fact, during his lifetime, Nicolaus Copernicus was employed as a canon in the cathedral in Frauenberg, Germany, a sinecure that permitted him time for his studies.

Born in Poland in 1473, Copernicus first studied mathematics and optics at the University of Kraków, and later canon law in Bologna, Italy. While in Bologna he met and studied under the astronomer Domenico Maria de

Novara, who taught him about the subject that was to become his main interest. He completed his education in medicine at Padua and gained a degree in canon law from Ferrara. Copernicus's uncle—Lucas Watzenrode, who was soon to become the Bishop of Warmia—arranged his nephew's position as a canon in Frauenberg, which he combined with practicing medicine at the episcopal court.

At the time, general understanding of astronomy was linked to the Ptolemaic and Aristotelian theories, both of which involved the earth being the center of the universe—the "geocentric" model. Making observations with the naked eye from a turret on the walls of Frauenberg Cathedral, Copernicus came to a different conclusion. He proposed that the sun was near the center of the universe, and this enabled him to explain the earth's rotation daily on its axis and annually around the sun—a hugely radical proposition in the religious and scientific climate of the time. In 1514 he wrote the "Little Commentary," containing seven principles outlining this theory, which was distributed narrowly to a few friends and colleagues.

In the same year, Copernicus was consulted by the Fifth Lateran Council on the subject of possible reform of the calendar. The authorities recognized that the calendar system then in use was not correct, and Copernicus's advice was sought as he was seen as an authority on astronomical observation. In reply, however, he stated that he did not feel that his studies were far enough advanced yet to alter the system. In fact, at the time Copernicus was working on a groundbreaking book that contained his expanded theory of a "heliocentric" (sun-oriented) view of the solar system—but such a theory had theological as well as scientific implications, so it is little wonder that he was cautious about making it public.

Astronomical calculations were necessary to determine the dating of religious festivals such as Easter in the calendar, and also the position of individual planets relative to each other. These were complicated using the existing geocentric model, but much easier with Copernicus's heliocentric theory. Copernicus's book was eventually published as *De Revolutionibus*, and dedicated to Pope Paul III, but it had taken the intervention of a Lutheran scholar, George Rheticus—who stayed with Copernicus for two years—to persuade him to publish the work.

The responsibility for printing the book was given to Andreas Osiander, who took it upon himself to add a preface in an attempt to make the book more acceptable to the Church—the preface suggested that the results were not presented as the truth, but were intended to simplify calculations. A finished copy of *De Revolutionibus* was reportedly handed to Copernicus on his deathbed in 1543, and it is possible that he may not have noticed the amendment.

Opposition by the Church to the book did not materialize until 1616, after Galileo had made reference to Copernicus's work in his own writing. *De Revolutionibus* was placed on the Church's index of prohibited books in 1616 and was only removed in 1835. However, Kohler and Langdon appear to be off the mark in claiming that the Church had Copernicus murdered. There is no evidence to suggest that was the case: his death seems to have been due to a stroke.

See also: Galileo Galilei.

Cross, The

These days the cross is regarded as the principal symbol of
the Christian religion, signifying the crucifixion, Passion,
and death of Jesus Christ. However, its use as an icon for
Christ and his suffering was rare during the first three
centuries after his death. The Emperor Constantine, who
adopted Christianity as the state religion of Rome in the
fourth century, actually used the Chi-Rho monogram on his
banner, which was more common at the time. The Chi-Rho
(named for the first two letters of Christ's name in
Greek) was added to the military standard that was
carried into battle, originally called the *vexillum* and
later known as the *labarum*. It was only into the third
century that the cross became widely used as a Christian
symbol and icon; the theologian Clement of Alexandria
called it "the symbol of the Lord."

Today Catholics and orthodox Christians make the sign
of the cross with their right hand, a gesture that has been
common practice as far back as the time of St Augustine in
the seventh century.

It was the Emperor Constantine's mother, Helena, whose
pilgrimage to locate the True Cross of Christ helped to
promote the symbol's importance at the heart of the
Christian religion in the fourth century. According to
medieval legend, the True Cross of Christ was made from
the Tree of Jesse (named for the father of King David)—this
tree later became identified with the Tree of Knowledge in
the Garden of Eden.

In *Angels & Demons*, Dan Brown uses the sign of the
cross to indicate a link between the four places where the
cardinals are murdered. However, Brown has somewhat
distorted his map of Rome to make his imaginary cross
uniform and straight. A cursory glance at the map in the
plates section of this book will give you a more accurate
idea of the cross shape that emerges.

See also: Rome.

Dollar-Bill Symbolism

All American one-dollar bills currently in circulation originated from a design that first came off the presses in 1957. It was then that the phrase "In God We Trust" was first used on paper money, although it had been in use on coinage for some time. The paper used in the one-dollar bill is actually a material mixture, made from cotton and linen, with tiny red and blue silk fibres running through it. It is printed with a secret blend of ink and overprinted with the symbols we see today, before being starched and made water-resistant, then pressed to give it a crisp feel. The face of George Washington stares from the front of the bill, alongside the Seal of the US Treasury, with its scales and key symbols. And on the reverse of the note is the Great Seal.

In the novel, Robert Langdon explains to Vittoria Vetra that the reason he first became interested in the Illuminati was because of the symbolism he noticed on the reverse of the dollar bill. They discuss the image of the pyramid and the eye, and Langdon remarks that the insignia was significant in Illuminati philosophy. So, did the design come from Illuminati symbolism? And if not, where *did* it come from?

The formal US Government explanation for the symbolism on the Great Seal of the United States—the official symbol of the nation, representing its strength and fortitude—is as follows:

> The Great Seal was first used on the reverse of the one-dollar Federal Reserve note in 1935. The Department of State is the official keeper of the Seal. They believe that the most accurate explanation of a pyramid on the Great Seal is that it symbolizes strength and durability. The unfinished pyramid means that the United States will always grow, improve and build. In addition, the "All-Seeing Eye" located above the pyramid suggests the importance of divine guidance in favor of the American cause.
>
> The inscription ANNUIT COEPTIS translates as

"He (God) has favored our undertakings," and refers to the many instances of Divine Providence during our Government's formation. In addition, the inscription NOVUS ORDO SECLORUM translates as "A new order of the ages," and signifies a new American era.

It was a US Government minister, Henry Agard Wallace, who first decided to print the Great Seal on the dollar bill. Wallace, who would later go on to become Vice-President of the United States from 1940 to 1944 under President Franklin D. Roosevelt, was undoubtedly a Freemason and held Masonic beliefs that have led many to speculate that he used the Great Seal to signify his convictions on a national level. A biography of Wallace written by US political journalist Dwight Macdonald notes that, "Just as Wallace thinks of America as the nation destined by God to lead the world, so Wallace thinks of himself as a Messiah, an instrument through whom God will guide America onward and upward." Wallace himself made these comments about the significance of the Grand Seal in 1934: "It will take a more definite recognition of the Grand Architect of the Universe before the apex stone [the missing capstone of the symbolic pyramid] is finally fitted into place and this nation in the full strength of its power is in position to assume leadership among the nations in inaugurating 'the New Order of the Ages.'"

It would seem, then, that the use of the Great Seal on the dollar bill is steeped in Masonic symbolism and meaning. But the Great Seal existed long before its appearance on the dollar bill. And the symbol's roots have long been entwined with the history of Freemasonry in the United States.

Many researchers claim that the founding fathers of the United States were all practicing Freemasons. These claims are difficult to substantiate and have been refuted by official Masonic sources. However, prominent Mason and writer on the esoteric, Manly P. Hall (who allegedly rose to the rank of 33rd-degree member of the order), is quoted as saying, "Of the fifty-five members of the Constitutional Convention, all but five were Masons." What we know for certain is that George Washington, the first President of the United States, was undoubtedly a Freemason, and wore the symbol of the eye in the pyramid emblazoned on his Masonic apron. Of the other founding fathers, Benjamin Franklin was also a Freemason. These two were members of the first committee assigned to design and implement the Great Seal of the United States. Their first efforts included the motif of the all-seeing eye, but they were otherwise unsuccessful. Eventually the symbols we see today were incorporated into the Great Seal by Charles Thompson, who was the Secretary of Congress in 1782, and William Barton, although it is not known whether or not these two were Masons. Thompson is reported as telling Congress that the pyramid represented "Strength and Duration." The eye symbol, sitting atop the pyramid in the triangular apex stone, has long been a Masonic icon, and signifies divinity and the all-seeing eye of the Great Lord of the Universe; the pyramid itself has its western side in shadow, and some researchers claim this represented the darkness in the West of the country, which had not been explored at this time. The eagle on the Great Seal serves as the basis for the symbol of office for the President of the United States, the bald eagle being chosen as a symbol of victory and strength. The Great Seal was officially established by Congress on June 20, 1782.

According to conspiracy theorists, the dollar-bill symbolism is a flag bearer for the Illuminati—the grand cabal behind allegedly everything. They claim that this is evidence of a brilliant and manipulative scheme—its instigators blatantly placed the icons of Illuminati power in front of everyone's eyes.

The truth, it would seem, is a little less sensational. It is fair to say that the Great Seal does incorporate Masonic symbols; some of the founding fathers were Masons; and Henry Wallace, who had the Great Seal included on the dollar bill, was definitely a dedicated Mason. But this proves nothing more than the fact that these individuals were people of their time, members of Masonic orders when it was a natural thing for men of a certain standing to be so.

However, as an interesting aside, one striking feature of the United States one-dollar bill is the repeated occurrence of the number 13. On the pyramid in the Great Seal there are 13 steps; there are 13 letters in the phrase above the pyramid (ANNUIT COEPTIS);13 letters in the Latin phrase E PLURIBUS UNUM ("One [nation] from many [people]") held in the beak of the eagle of the Great Seal; there are 13 stars above the eagle; 13 leaves on the olive branch that the eagle holds; 13 bars on the shield that the eagle is behind; 13 plumes of feathers on each span of the eagle's wing; and 13 arrows are held in the eagle's other talon. Moreover, at the time of the signing of the Declaration of Independence, 13 colonies were represented, which are symbolized by the 13 stripes on the flag of the United States. In some occultist circles the number 13 is seen as representing Satan, but in traditional Masonic symbolism the number 13 is a power number, signifying strength.

See also: Freemasonry; Illuminati; Knights Templar; New World Order.

Ecstasy of St Teresa, The

Bernini's masterpiece depicts the encounter between St Teresa and an angel, and is to be found in the Cornaro Chapel within the Church of Santa Maria della Vittoria in Rome. It is the site of the third cardinal's murder in *Angels & Demons*, and is associated with the element of fire. The statue shows the moment St Teresa was awakened by the angel, which she described thus:

> . . . fine angels that seem to be made of light [Author's note: this appears to be an allusion to what some commentators have called a seraph or "burning one"]. I saw a long golden dart in his hands, and it seemed to me that there was a touch of fire on its point. It seemed as if he wounded my heart several times with it and that it penetrated my viscera; and when he drew it out, it was as if he took them away. The pain was so real that I uttered little cries; but the sweetness produced by this intense pain is so great that you wish it would never cease . . .

The ecstatic language of St Teresa's account, and the sensuous nature of the sculpture, led Robert Langdon to spend a few moments considering the sexual overtones of the work. Cardinal Federico Cornaro, who commissioned Bernini to decorate the family chapel in which the statue resides, may not have been expecting its centerpiece still to be exciting speculation over three centuries later. However, it seems clear from St Teresa's language that she is indeed alluding to a sexual experience, as some researchers have suggested.

Bernini had experience as a stage designer, and he brought the theatrical to this design. The marble statue stands about 11 feet (3.4m) in height and is lit by reflected light from a hidden window, which adds luminosity to the figures. Along both sides of the chapel, Bernini has placed statues depicting members of the Cornaro family in theater boxes, to view the spectacle.

Bernini created the chapel and its statue in the years 1647–51, when St Teresa had only recently been canonized. After acknowledging her vocation, Teresa of Avila had entered a Carmelite convent. She suffered severe health problems and experienced visions that she described in the account of her spiritual life. She confided in her fellow nuns, who persuaded her that her visions were a gift from God. Her memory of the encounter with the seraph described above became a lifelong influence. St Teresa used it to understand the suffering and endurance of Jesus, and it inspired a motto—"Lord, either let me suffer or let me die"—that is often inscribed on her images. When she died in 1582, her body was preserved, and she was canonized in 1622 by Pope Gregory XV.

See also: Bernini, Gian Lorenzo; Santa Maria della Vittoria.

Egyptian Religion

While inside the Pantheon, Robert Langdon notices a Christian tomb oddly out of line with the orientation of the building. It reminds him of one of his recent symbology lectures concerning the way Christianity borrowed from ancient Egyptian religion, particularly with regard to the sun.

Despite its large number of gods and goddesses, Egyptian religion remained consistent for 2,600 years. The ancient Egyptians realized that both order and chaos needed to exist side by side. Each was vital to the existence of the other, which is why gods that we would consider evil were worshiped and their temples and priesthood held in high regard. In order to maintain the status quo it was vital that chaos did not overrun life. This was achieved by upholding the principles of Maat (truth).

Religion was, therefore, intrinsic to all things in ancient Egyptian life. It incorporated prayer, magic, and medicine, and it was perfectly normal to treat an illness using all of these elements. Each aspect was considered as important and necessary as the other, as each sought to control chaos/evil and restore Maat. Disease might be attributed to neglect of the gods or to blasphemy, and could be cured by acts of penitence.

Egyptian deities can be roughly divided into national gods (e.g. Ra, Osiris, Horus), local gods, and household gods. State religion concentrated heavily upon kingship and the needs of the state, as shown by temple reliefs that depict the pharaoh killing Egypt's enemies, fighting battles, and making offerings to the gods. The concerns of everyday religion concentrated on the priorities of the ordinary person and the necessity of protecting themselves against disease and harm. Household gods underline this concern—the hippopotamus goddess Taweret protected women in childbirth, and the dwarf god Bes brought good luck for the family as well as helping women in labor. Children were often given protective amulets to wear as necklaces. To help an individual's cause, prayers were also offered up to the dead, or written on bowls and placed within tombs. It was believed that the deceased could intercede on a person's behalf in order to right a wrong.

Ra, the creator sun god, was the supreme deity. Ra's journey across the sky each day represented a new creation and resurrection of his body after his journey through the Underworld at night. In whatever guise he was given, the sun god held a central place in the moment of creation. To the people of ancient Egypt, creation (which, in ancient Egyptian, translated literally as "first time") occurred when a mound of earth emerged from the primeval waters. From this sacred ground the sun god emerged and his life-giving force resulted in the creation of all things. The *benben* stone was a sacred stone that represented this moment and was linked to the sun god. From this stone the obelisk developed, another object closely associated with the Egyptian cult of the sun. Everything created at the "first time" was perfect, and everything that came after sought to emulate that perfection.

At the city of Heliopolis ("sun city" in Greek) the sun god was embodied in the form of Atum ("the All"). He too was a sun god responsible for creation and his ensuing dynasty made up the Ennead (Nine) of Heliopolis, the keystone of Egyptian religious literature.

Another important creator god was Amun-Ra. He created matter from nothingness using the forces of *Heka* (magic), *Sia* (perception), and *Hu* (the divine word). Even in this tradition, creation is linked with the sun, as Amun-Ra—as his name suggests—was also a sun god.

It was common for important Egyptian deities to merge together in order to combine their various aspects for specific purposes. Deities also took on different guises according to their role. Therefore, the great goddess Isis became the goddess Hathor (meaning "the womb of Horus," her son) when she adopted the role of motherhood. In this guise she took the form of a cow. However, a deity could commonly have very different, even opposite, attributes. As well as being the cow of motherhood, Hathor is the goddess whom Ra sent out to destroy mankind.

A temporary change in the ancient Egyptian religion occurred under the pharaoh Akhenaten (ruled 1379–62 BC), who worshiped the Aten or sun-disk. The Aten was the sole creator god, and as such was the only source of life and the only god. At this time the other gods were banished and monuments that featured them were defaced. Akhenaten decreed that the Aten could only be accessed through the king, and he commissioned artworks that displayed the Aten's life-giving sun rays stretching out to the pharaoh and his family. However, on Akhenaten's death the old religion was revived and the ancient gods once again took their places within their temples.

The cult of Isis and Osiris spread to the Mediterranean and beyond, so that in later periods their temples can be found as far afield as Athens and London. Isis and Serapis (originally a separate deity, who came to be seen as another aspect of Osiris) became so popular in ancient Rome that a large temple was built in the city, at which an obelisk was erected by the Emperor Domitian. This obelisk is now the centerpiece of the *Fountain of the Four Rivers*, still in Rome, at which Langdon encounters the Hassassin.

In spite of the persecution suffered by their followers, Isis and Osiris became the focus of a mysterious cult popular throughout the Hellenistic world and the Roman Empire. The appeal of Isis was the result of her universal qualities, and her cult rivaled Christianity for dominance for some time. Indeed, certain aspects of Christianity can trace their origins back to the cult of Isis and Osiris. In AD 140 the Roman writer Apuleius described Isis as the "eternal savior," a term Christians also ascribed to Jesus. Osiris was closely connected with the resurrection of the dead, and after his own death he rose on the third day, just as Jesus did. Similarly, the concept of the holy family found a parallel in Osiris, Isis, and Horus, while the image of Mary and Jesus as mother and child has a direct predecessor in Isis and Horus, who sits on his mother's lap. Certain qualities and titles attributed to the Virgin Mary were also characteristic of Isis. Moreover, her followers practiced baptism by water after confession of their sins, and believed in the forgiveness of sin through repentance, and in an eternal afterlife—all important tenets of the later Christian faith.

Many alternative scholars hold the view that the Egyptian religion played a significant role in the teachings of Jesus, and suggest that Jesus was either heavily influenced by it or that he was not Jewish but an adherent to the Egyptian religion (see Morton Smith, *Jesus the Magician*).

It has even been suggested that Jesus and Mary Magdalene were initiates of the Osiris/Isis cult. In *The Templar Revelation*, Lynn Picknett and Clive Prince have suggested that Jesus was crucified as part of an Osirian resurrection enactment to achieve enlightenment. They consider Jesus to have been an initiate of the Egyptian religion, with his teachings adapted to suit the Jewish traditions of the time. In his book *Egyptian Light and Hebrew Fire*, Karl W. Luckert calls Christianity the "daughter born of Mother Egypt," along with "her ancient Hebrew paternal tradition."

Certainly in *Angels & Demons* Langdon and Vittoria discover a surprising number of ancient Egyptian symbols such as pyramids and obelisks in their travels around the Christian capital of Rome—occurrences which Langdon attributes to the influence of the Illuminati.

See also: Fountain of the Four Rivers; Obelisks.

Einstein, Albert

If we remember nothing else from our physics lessons, most of us will recognize the equation $E=MC^2$, and associate it with Albert Einstein. In *Angels & Demons* Vittoria Vetra recalls with fondness how her father, the late Leonardo Vetra, tried to teach her about Einstein's science in her childhood, though CERN director Maximilian

Kohler makes the rather ambitious claim that she has "disproved one of Einstein's fundamental theories" with her marine observations.

Einstein's early years were not marked by conspicuous academic achievement. He was born in Germany in 1879 and his interest in science was encouraged by two uncles, one of whom showed him a compass. Einstein realized that something in the "empty" space was influencing the needle to move, and he later looked back on the occasion as a significant moment for him. His education was completed in Switzerland, after which he obtained work in the Swiss Patent Office, continuing his researches into theoretical physics in his spare time.

In 1905 Einstein produced four articles, one of which— on the subject of photoelectric effect—was to win him a Nobel Prize in 1921. Another of the four, "On the Electrodynamics of Moving Bodies," introduced the Special Theory of Relativity. This is the theory connecting time, distance, energy, and mass, and it drew on Galileo's idea that the laws of nature should be the same for all observers that move with constant speed relative to each other.

In his paper "Does the Inertia of a Body Depend Upon its Energy Content?" Einstein makes a further deduction that leads to the equation $E=MC^2$. This important equation, which makes it possible to calculate the amount of energy released in nuclear fission, was to be instrumental in the development of nuclear weapons. In later life Einstein was a pacifist and campaigned against future use of atomic weapons—in much the same way as, in *Angels & Demons*, Vittoria and her father fear the deadly possibilities of their discovery of how to create and store antimatter.

From 1914 to 1933, Einstein lived in Berlin and worked at the Kaiser Wilhelm Institute, although he traveled widely and supported the Zionist cause, raising money for the Palestine Foundation Fund. On a visit to the Mount Wilson

Observatory in the San Gabriel Mountains in California, he heard Georges Lemaître describe his big bang theory of the origin of the universe, which Einstein enthusiastically described as "the most beautiful and satisfactory explanation of creation to which I have ever listened."

After the rise of Hitler, Einstein moved to the United States, where he held a position at the Institute for Advanced Study in Princeton, New Jersey. There he worked toward the development of a unified field theory of relativity, which attempted to link the fundamental forces of nature (gravitational fields, electromagnetic fields, and strong and weak nuclear interactions).

In 1952, the state of Israel offered Einstein the opportunity to become its second president, an offer he declined. He had once observed that "Politics are for the moment, an equation is for eternity," and since his death in 1955, his famous equation has certainly granted him eternal recognition.

See also: Antimatter; Big Bang Theory; Galileo Galilei.

Fountain of the Four Rivers

In *Angel & Demons,* the *Fountain of the Four Rivers* is the site of a confrontation between Robert Langdon and the Hassassin, after Langdon has anticipated where water, the final element, will be represented. It provides the murder scene for the last of the unfortunate cardinals, who is drowned in the waters that surround the sculpted figures and the obelisk in the center of the fountain.

The fountain is located in the elegant Piazza Navona, created in the 1640s by Pope Innocent X on the site once occupied by a stadium built by the Roman Emperor Domitian. Innocent X came from the Pamphili family, whose impressive Palazzo Pamphili, decorated by Francesco Borromini, occupies one side of the square. The Pope decided to redirect a reserve of water from the *acqua vergine*, one of Rome's principal water supplies, to enable Bernini to create the fountain.

Work on the figures representing the four main rivers of the world was mostly undertaken by Bernini's students; it is thought that the master was responsible for carving some of the designs, however, including a horse, a palm tree, and a lion. The four rivers, one from each continent known at the time, are analogous to the four biblical rivers of Paradise. They are: the Danube, representing Europe; the Ganges, representing Asia; the Nile, representing Africa—shown with the figure's head covered, as the source was not then known to Europeans; and the Rio de la Plata, representing the Americas, and depicted with coins to show the wealth that continent was believed to hold.

Rising from the travertine and marble rock of the fountain base is a red granite obelisk that extends 52 feet (15.8m) into the air, and is topped by a statue of a dove. The obelisk was quarried in Aswan, Egypt, for the Emperor Domitian, probably to mark his accession in AD 81. It was originally erected in Rome between the temples of Serapis and Isis (who were worshiped in Rome as well as in their native Egypt), was moved to the Circus de Massenzio—where it toppled over—and years later was reclaimed by Innocent X as part of his grand design. The obelisk surrounded by waters is an echo of the annual inundation (flooding) of the Nile in Egypt. It has also been suggested that the scene might symbolically represent Mount Ararat as the biblical flood subsides, with the dove of peace coming to rest on the top of the obelisk.

In fact, the dove was the family symbol of the Pamphili family, whose name in Greek breaks down to *pan* (everybody) and *filios* (lover, or friend)—i.e. "everybody's friend." It may have been for this reason that the family adopted the dove, messenger of peace and friendship, as its emblem.

In the novel, Robert Langdon accomplishes the considerable feat of climbing the fountain to the level of the platform base of the obelisk, so that he can follow the direction in which the dove is pointing. Even to reach the base would necessitate a difficult ascent up smooth cut stone, so any attempt to recreate this action would no doubt provide amusement to the patrons of the many cafés that line the piazza.

See also: Bernini, Gian Lorenzo; Egyptian Religion; Obelisks.

Freemasonry

Robert Langdon claims that the organization we know as the Order of Freemasons was used to shield members of the Illuminati when they were being persecuted by the Church. He further suggests that the aims he attributes to the Illuminati, such as the obliteration of the Catholic Church, were subversively introduced into Freemasonry. In order to understand why this suggestion should be made in the novel, we need to examine the brotherhood of Freemasons in greater detail.

With an estimated 4 million Freemasons worldwide and more than 60,000 books written on the subject, this so-called "secret" society must be one of the best-known organizations in the world. Over the last three centuries their fraternity has included American presidents, senators, and chief justices, British prime ministers, members of the British royal family, army generals, and police chiefs. Many critics have attacked

Freemasonry for being a "secret society," but Freemasonry prefers to call itself "a society with secrets."

The earliest origins of Freemasonry remain shrouded in mystery despite years of extensive research by Freemason historians, conspiracy theorists, and alternative-history authors. Activities in the early years of Freemasonry (believed to be during the fourteenth century) were very poorly recorded, so reliable documentary evidence simply does not exist. As historical facts are few, there has been much wild speculation and many legends regarding the society's origins.

Some theories abound that ancient secret knowledge (such as alchemical wisdom and sacred geometry) was passed on to the early Masons by refugee Knights Templar (a controversial order of Christian monks), who fled to Scotland in 1307 after they had suffered persecution by the Church. However, there is no historical evidence whatsoever to support this belief. There was no safe haven for the Templars in Scotland: the order was brought to trial in Edinburgh in 1309; and there were no "refugee Templars" riding with the Scots at the Battle of Bannockburn.

The more prosaic but widely accepted explanation for the origins of Freemasonry is that it grew out of the craft guild traditions of medieval stonemasons. When the castles, cathedrals, and churches of Europe were being constructed in the Middle Ages, skilled stonemasons were highly regarded artisans. Building sites have always been dangerous places and stonemasons did not have life insurance to protect their families in the event of an accident, so they formed themselves into groups that would look after the families of members who were killed or incapacitated. These stonemasons were known as "operative" masons: professional craftsman and artisans. To ensure that a traveling stonemason was genuinely as skilled and experienced as he claimed, a series of secret signs, passwords, and rules were devised so that masons could recognize one another.

Modern Freemasonry continues to use terms that have their origins in medieval stonemasonry. For example, Freemasons meet in "lodges." Today Masonic lodges are often grand buildings with vast meeting halls, marble statuary, and antique furniture. In the days of the medieval craft guilds, however, a stonemason's lodge was a small temporary wooden hut that was built up against the wall of a building as it was under construction. This lodge gave the masons shelter from the rain and snow, as well as a place to meet. Modern lodges have at their head an officer known as the "Worshipful Master." "Worshipful" in this context simply means "highly respected" and "Master" means "best qualified"—as in the master mason, who would have been the most skilled and experienced man on a medieval building site.

At some point non-masons were allowed to join the lodges of the stonemasons. These individuals were known as "speculative masons" and were effectively honorary members. In time these working guilds evolved into fraternal groups of "freemasons."

On June 24—the feast day of St John—in the year 1717, the first ever Grand Lodge was formed in Britain. Four of the lodges that had been operating independently in London came together to create a single organization that would oversee administration and policy-making for Masonic lodges. Freemasonry grew rapidly in Europe and crossed the Atlantic to the North American colonies in the 1730s. Initially Freemasonry expanded very slowly in North America. Then, in the mid-eighteenth century, the brotherhood began to grow rapidly, and dozens of new lodges sprang up.

Many of the leaders of the American colonists during the War of Independence were Freemasons, including Benjamin Franklin and General Lafayette. It should also be

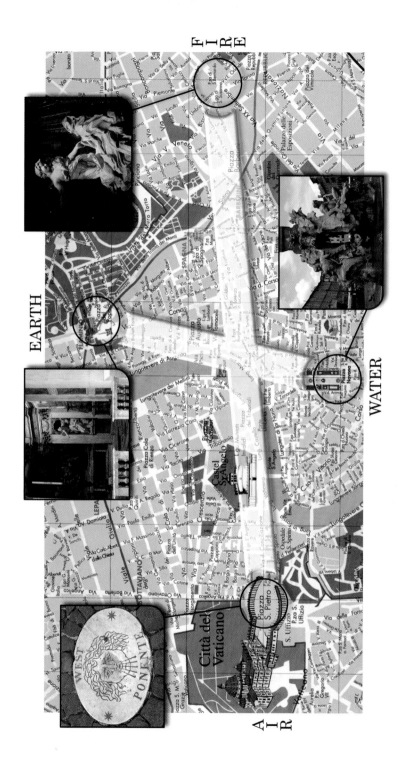

(*Above*) The heart of the Catholic Church and the seat of the papacy, the Vatican provides the backdrop for much of the action in *Angels & Demons*. It is built on the spot where St Peter was reputedly martyred.

(*Left*) The Vatican's security services are provided by the Swiss Guards, widely regarded as the world's most loyal foot soldiers.

(*Previous page*) This map of Rome shows the locations of the four murders in *Angels & Demons*.

(*Right*) Raphael Santi, Renaissance artist and architect of the Chigi Chapel in Rome. Raphael was also responsible for producing frescoes for the papal apartments in the Vatican.

(*Below*) The Pantheon in Rome houses the tomb of Raphael, the site where Robert Langdon believes the first murder will take place. It is claimed that the extraordinary hole in the ceiling was created by demons fleeing when the church was consecrated.

(*Left*) Gian Lorenzo Bernini, Italian sculptor and father of the Baroque. Was he also a secret member of the Illuminati?

(*Left*) Bernini's *Habakkuk and the Angel* stands in Raphael's Chigi Chapel, in the Church of Santa Maria del Popolo, the site of the first cardinal's murder in *Angels & Demons.*

(*Right*) Bernini's *West Ponente* or "Breath of God," set into the pavement blocks in St Peter's Square, depicts the West Wind. It is also the site of the second cardinal's murder in *Angels & Demons*.

(*Below*) Bernini's masterpiece, *The Ecstasy of St Teresa*, represents the element of fire in *Angels & Demons*, and marks the location of the third cardinal's death. Based on Teresa's own writings, the sculpture is shrouded in controversy due to its sexually explicit imagery.

(*Left*) The *Fountain of the Four Rivers*, located in Piazza Navona, symbolizes the element of water, and is the setting of the murder of the last cardinal. Rising out of the fountain is an obelisk, one of the many "lofty pyramids" found throughout Rome.

(*Below*) Fatebenefratelli Hospital on the Isola Tiberina, an island that has been associated with healing since it was first inhabited by abandoned slaves in ancient times, and the site of Robert Langdon's treatment after his miraculous fall from the helicopter.

(*Above*) Originally built by Emperor Hadrian as a mausoleum, Castel Sant'Angelo became a refuge for popes during medieval times. Did it later become the Illuminati lair, as suggested in *Angels & Demons?*

(*Right*) One of Bernini's "Breezy Maniacs" on the Ponte Sant'Angelo, which helped to guide Robert Langdon in his quest to find the Hassassin. The statues are so named because of the way the angels' clothing is whipped by an invisible wind.

(*Left*) The Great Seal, which appears on the reverse of the US one-dollar bill, is noted for its Masonic symbolism. But does it also have connections with the Illuminati?

(*Below*) Galileo Galilei was an astronomer and physicist, whose scientific theories and beliefs led him into conflict with the Catholic Church. In *Angels & Demons* it is claimed that he was an instrumental member of the Illuminati brotherhood, but what are the facts?

noted, however, that the notorious traitor Benedict Arnold was a Freemason.

One of America's most famous Freemasons was George Washington, who joined the brethren in 1753. General George Washington was Commander-in-Chief of the colonists' forces in the American War of Independence. After the country gained its independence from Great Britain, it was suggested that Washington should be made King, but he was appalled by the notion and instead became the first American President. Contrary to popular belief, Washington was never a Grand Master Mason. The American Union Lodge had suggested that Washington become "General Grand Master" of a "National Grand Lodge," but the latter never came into existence; instead, each state retains its own Grand Lodge. When Washington died he was buried with Masonic rites.

Prominent Masons have long played an instrumental part in American history. Nine signatories of the Declaration of Independence in 1776, including Benjamin Franklin and John Hancock, were members of the society. Ten of the signatories of the Articles of Confederation in 1777 were Freemasons. And there were thirteen Freemasons among the signatories of the Constitution of the United States in 1788.

Freemasonry can be said to have a real, albeit mysterious, history and a parallel "legendary" history. Masonic legends are allegorical: they are stories that have symbolic meaning but are not intended to be taken literally. Freemasonry's most important foundation legend tells of Hiram Abif, the Architect of Solomon's Temple in Jerusalem. Hiram appears in the Old Testament, in the first Book of Kings and in Chronicles. The Bible relates that when King Solomon decided to build his temple, he approached the King of Tyre, who sent cedars from Lebanon for materials and an architect named Hiram. Masonic legend expands upon this basic story, telling us that Hiram was a master mason who had special esoteric knowledge. He was attacked by three journeymen who demanded to know his secrets. Hiram refused to reveal what he knew. The three journeymen murdered him with a blow to the head and hid his body in a secret place. This legend has become the central so-called "mystery" of Freemasonry. It is re-enacted in initiation rituals in Masonic lodges around the world as the degree of Master Mason is conferred.

Freemasonry has always attracted high-ranking officials and prominent men, and this has led to claims of Masonic conspiracies. When President John F. Kennedy was assassinated, for example, Vice-President Lyndon B. Johnson was quickly sworn in as his replacement and immediately ordered the Federal Bureau of Investigation to investigate the assassination. Johnson had received the Entered Apprentice Degree at a Masonic lodge in Texas in 1937. J. Edgar Hoover, the head of the FBI, had joined Federal Lodge No.1, District of Columbia, back in 1920. The Warren Commission was headed by Chief Justice Earl Warren, who was a past Grand Master, and two other commissioners were also known Freemasons: Representative (and future President) Gerald R. Ford and Senator Richard B. Russell. The coincidence of so many Freemasons heading the investigations into Kennedy's assassination has led to accusations of a cover-up.

Other Freemasons who have served as American presidents include James Monroe, Andrew Jackson—who served as a Grand Master of Masons—James Knox Polk, James Buchanan, Andrew Johnson, James A. Garfield, William McKinley, Theodore Roosevelt, William Howard Taft, Warren G. Harding, and Franklin D. Roosevelt (another Grand Master). Harry S. Truman was a Grand Master, and was also made a Sovereign Grand Inspector General, 33rd Degree, and Honorary Member of the Supreme Council. He was also elected an Honorary Grand Master of the International Supreme Council of the Order of De Molay. In 1959 he reached his golden anniversary in Freemasonry and was presented with a 50-year award. President Ronald Reagan was not a Mason, but he was made an honorary member of the Imperial Council of the Shrine—a body within the Freemasons—and was often involved in Masonic functions.

Surprisingly, neither former president George Bush Sr nor his son President George W. Bush is a Freemason. George Bush Sr took the oath of office on the George Washington Bible, which belongs to the St John's Lodge in New York City, when he was sworn in at his inauguration, and many authors have assumed he is a Freemason because this bible belongs to a Masonic Lodge. In 1789 this bible was used by the Grand Master of the Masons in New York to administer the oath of office to George Washington, the first US president.

It is perhaps worth considering why so many influential and powerful men have been attracted to the brotherhood throughout history. Essentially, becoming a member of the organization gives like-minded ambitious men the opportunity to make valuable contacts, which can serve them well both professionally and socially. Being a Freemason is not unlike being part of an elite club, where introductions to other members can be mutually beneficial in the worlds of business and politics.

Other famous Freemasons include: the former British prime minister Sir Winston Churchill; King Edward VII; King Edward VIII; King George VI; the second man on the moon, Edwin "Buzz" Aldrin; the creator of Sherlock Holmes, Sir Arthur Conan Doyle; the composers Ludwig van Beethoven and Wolfgang Amadeus Mozart; the movie actors Clark Gable and John Wayne; the founder of Hilton Hotels, Charles C. Hilton; the founder of Kentucky Fried Chicken, Harland "Colonel" Sanders; and former US general and Desert Storm commander, Norman Schwarzkopf.

See also: Dollar-Bill Symbolism; Illuminati; Knights Templar; New World Order.

Gaea

The name of Gaea, goddess of the earth, crops up when Robert Langdon and Vittoria Vetra discuss different belief systems on their plane trip from CERN to Rome. Vittoria links the Native American understanding of a mother earth with Gaea, as does Langdon when considering the pagan gods associated with the Pantheon in Rome.

In Greek mythology Gaea represented the fertility of the earth, and was a derivation of the figure of the mother goddess, which had been worshiped since Neolithic times. Gaea could be identified as a combination of Demeter (the mother), Persephone (the daughter), and Hecate (the crone). In the Anatolia region, now part of Turkey, she was known as Cybele. The figure of Gaea was a mother, a nurse, and a nourisher of children, her legend giving her many consorts and offspring including the Titans, a group of twelve gods who challenged the authority of Zeus and the Olympian gods in a violent struggle.

The Romans, who tended to acquire deities as their empire spread, associated Cybele with Magna Mater, the Great Mother (i.e. mother earth). Altars were erected to her on the site of what is now the second largest Christian building in the world, St Peter's Basilica in Rome. (The Basilica of Our Lady of Peace in Ivory Coast, West Africa, became the largest on its completion in 1989.)

See also: Pantheon, The; Rome; St Peter's Basilica.

Galileo Galilei

The great sixteenth-century Italian scientist Galileo Galilei spent many years under house arrest because his views were in conflict with the teachings of the Catholic Church. Dan Brown has suggested that Galileo played an instrumental part in a secret organization, the Illuminati, comprising artists and scientists opposed to the Church. What makes Galileo a candidate for this role?

Galileo was born on February 15, 1564, in Pisa, Italy, into a noble family that had declined in fortune. After attending a monastery school in Vallombrosa he began to study medicine at the university in Pisa, but showed little aptitude for the subject. By 1583 he was immersed in mathematics and philosophy and was studying physics according to the Greek philosopher Aristotle. However, Galileo's experiments with objects falling or rolling down an inclined plane called the Aristotelian model into question, and from 1589-92 he gathered his own theories in the manuscript *De Motu* ("On Motion"). Famously, he had used Pisa's leaning tower as the platform for his experiments in dropping items from different heights. Another landmark discovery in 1602 was that the length of time a pendulum takes to swing is not related to the arc of the swing—a fact Galileo was reputed to have discovered after observing a suspended lamp in Pisa Cathedral.

This early work was not related to the astronomy for which he is now famous, but Galileo went on to develop studies using the telescope he adapted to improve magnification, and he published *Siderius Nuncius* (*Sidereal Messenger*—"sidereal" meaning "related to the stars") in 1610. The book was dedicated to Grand Duke Cosimo de Medici, who by this time had become a patron of the scientist. Once again Galileo's work called Aristotle's theories into question, firstly in his assertion that the surface of the moon was not smooth, as the Greek philosopher had believed, but covered in valleys and mountains. More dramatically, the discovery that Jupiter was orbited by four moons (which Galileo called the *Sidera Medicea*—the Medicean stars) challenged the view that the earth was the center of motion for all heavenly bodies—an assertion that was to have serious consequences for Galileo's relationship with the Church. Traditional Aristotelian/Ptolemaic cosmology suffered two further challenges with Galileo's observation of the phases of Venus and the discovery of sunspots. These developments were not just of interest to the scientific community—at around that time the Tuscan painter Ludovico Cigoli included a contoured moon in a painting of the Virgin, which was placed in a church in Rome.

When Galileo's adapted telescope enabled him to observe vast numbers of small stars, he was able to confirm Copernicus's view that the universe was larger than previously believed. It was Copernicus who had first suggested that the earth orbits the sun, rather than the other way around, and it was to be Galileo's adoption of Copernican views that was to cause him his later problems.

In a letter to a pupil, Benedetto Castelli, in 1613, Galileo discussed the problem of reconciling scientific facts with biblical interpretation. Inaccurate copies of this letter were passed to the Inquisition (an ecclesiastical tribunal created for the suppression of heresy) and Galileo was ordered to Rome to explain himself. He had by then expanded his letter in a version to Grand Duchess Christina, his patron's mother, again highlighting the difficulty of squaring scientific discoveries with traditional biblical ideas.

Cardinal Bellarmine, who was set the task of investigating the question of possible heresy on Galileo's part, decided merely to warn the scientist that he should not promote Copernican views. Maffeo Barberini, a cardinal with an interest in science, argued against strong punishment for Galileo, and when he became Pope Urban VIII, Galileo may have expected a sympathetic supporter.

Indeed, initially Urban VIII agreed that Galileo could write about Copernican theory as long as his argument remained clearly hypothetical, a loophole through which Galileo gratefully attempted to slip.

In 1630 he wrote *Dialogue Concerning the Two Chief World Systems*, in the form of a discussion between three men: one representing himself, one holding Aristotelian views, and one an intelligent layman. Theories and arguments from the three different viewpoints were aired, and Galileo may have thought that he had been sufficiently subtle to get away with putting forward his radical ideas. It was not to be so. His work was found to contravene the injunction taken out against him in 1616, and he was forced to defend himself before the Inquisition. He tried semantics when charged with discussing Copernican views, producing a letter from the by now deceased Bellarmine that ordered him not to hold or defend the theory, but did not specifically forbid discussion. However, Galileo was declared guilty of heresy, ordered to recant his beliefs in the Copernican doctrine, and sentenced to life imprisonment. This was commuted to house arrest, and he was sent to his home near Florence, where eventually conditions were relaxed a little to permit him to receive visitors.

Undeterred, Galileo produced another major work in 1638—*Discourses on Two New Sciences*—which was smuggled out of Italy and published in Leiden, Holland. This may be the work Robert Langdon and Vittoria Vetra describe as *Discourses on the Tides* in *Angels & Demons*. Langdon also credits Galileo with a pamphlet published in 1639 called *Diagramma della Verità*, which contains the poem that can unlock the clues to the Illuminati's lair. While the presence of an obscure work by Galileo makes for heated speculation, the fictional *Diagramma* is not one of his attributed works.

Galileo became blind in later life and relied on a pupil to assist him. In 1638 he was visited by the English poet John Milton, who, inspired in part by Galileo's situation, later wrote a treatise on freedom of speech, known as his *Areopagitica*.

Despite never marrying, Galileo had three children with a Venetian woman named Marina Gamba. His two daughters entered convents, and the letters of one of them, Sister Marie Celeste, were recently published in Dava Sobel's book *Galileo's Daughter*.

After Galileo's death in 1642, the Church maintained its stance against him and the ecclesiastical authorities vetoed plans for a public funeral. Rehabilitation took a long time, despite many voices of support, and it was only in 1992 that the Roman Catholic Church finally admitted that the treatment of Galileo had been wrong and cleared him of heresy.

Galileo attracted the support of many within the Church, including a Benedictine abbot, his former pupil Benedetto Castelli, who continued to visit Galileo in his confinement. It is doubtful whether he would have attracted this support if serious suggestions existed at this time of Galileo's membership of an organization opposed to the Church. Unless further proof emerges, it is likely that the extent of Galileo's involvement with any fraternity such as the Illuminati will remain a mystery.

See also: Copernicus, Nicolaus; Illuminati; Milton, John.

Gatti, Annibale

Annibale Gatti is referred to in *Angels & Demons* as the nineteenth-century artist who painted a depiction of Galileo Galilei meeting the English poet John Milton. Milton is shown visiting Galileo at his home after his confinement there for heresy in his publications. Now housed in the Institute and Museum of the History of Science in Florence, the picture shows the two men deep in conversation, with one of Galileo's telescopes beside them on the table.

After moving to Florence in his youth, Gatti enrolled in the city's Academy of Fine Arts in 1843. Many of his works were commissions undertaken in conjunction with the architect Giuseppe Poggi, who was responsible for the restoration of many of Florence's old palaces. Gatti applied frescoes to the newly restored walls; he also decorated the ceiling of the Verdi Theater in Pisa.

See also: Galileo Galilei; Milton, John.

Habakkuk and the Angel

Armed with a clue directing them to "Santi's earthly tomb with demon's hole," Robert Langdon and Vittoria Vetra arrive at the Chigi Chapel, in the Church of Santa Maria del Popolo. The chapel contains a tomb designed by the artist Raphael Santi—better known to the world today simply as Raphael—for a rich local banker, Agostino Chigi.

The Chigi family was a wealthy dynasty, and the chapel was embellished further by Bernini, who added statues in niches to the sides of the chapel. This work was commissioned by Pope Alexander VII, who was the great nephew of Agostino, and whose name at birth was Fabio Chigi. Although the novel only mentions the statue *Habakkuk and the Angel*, there are in fact four sculptures by Bernini in the chapel, including one of Mary Magdalene—

a figure who played a significant role in the next novel by Dan Brown to feature Robert Langdon, *The Da Vinci Code*. In *Angels & Demons*, however, it is clear from the line "Let angels guide you on your lofty quest"—like the earlier quote above, also taken from the enigmatic poem in Galileo's *Diagramma* (an entirely fictional work, incidentally)—that it is the statue of *Habakkuk and the Angel* which holds the important clues, particularly the direction pointed to by the angel.

Habakkuk was an Old Testament prophet, and his story is found in the Book of Habakkuk, the eighth of the so-called books of Minor Prophets. The prophet was warned by God of a calamity that would come to the Judeans. In "Bel and the Dragon," a story contained within an Apocryphal book (i.e. a text that was not included in the Bible when it was being collated), Habakkuk is preparing a meal when an angel appears to him and instructs him to take the food to the prophet Daniel, who is in a lions' den in Babylon. Habakkuk protests that he has never been to Babylon and does not know where the lions' den is, whereupon the angel sweeps Habakkuk up by the hair, delivers both him and the meal to Daniel, and then returns Habakkuk to his home. Daniel, who was an interpreter of dreams, had been condemned to the lions' den for continuing to pray to God after the Babylonian King Darius had forbidden such worship. The lions left Daniel unharmed, and after releasing him the Babylonian king was moved to issue a decree honoring the "God of Daniel."

Bernini has depicted the pair at the moment in the story when the angel seizes Habakkuk by the hair to transport him to Babylon.

See also: Apocrypha; Bernini, Gian Lorenzo; Chigi Chapel; Raphael.

Hassassin

Better known as "Hashashin," or simply as the "Assassins," this notorious group of Arab killers have an interesting and unique history. The killer who commits the grisly murders of the cardinals in *Angels & Demons* considers himself to be descended from the Hassassin. In fact he makes the connection between his ancestors at the time of the Crusades and his own mission against the Church, which is fueled by a burning desire to seek revenge for the deaths of his Muslim antecedents, who were murdered at the hands of the Church's crusading armies from the eleventh to the thirteenth centuries AD.

Though the origins of the name are by no means clear, the word "assassin" is reputed to derive from the Arabic meaning "hashish smoker," which refers to the alleged practice of smoking hashish before and after a murder to induce ecstatic visions of an earthly paradise. These stories, in turn, are from legends which state that young inductees into the sect would take a liquid soporific of some kind, and wake to find themselves in a beautiful walled garden three days later. Here all the delights of an earthly paradise would be on offer to the young men, but after a certain time the potion would be readministered to them, and they would awake back in their homes. They would then be offered the task of assassinating a target, the prize for which would be a brief return to the garden if the task was successfully completed. If martyrdom ensued, their spirits would be taken to the garden to dwell for evermore.

Hasan-e-Sabbah (sometimes known as Hasan-i-Sabah) was a founder of the Nazari Isma'ilites, a religious and political Islamic sect that flourished in Persia and Syria from the eleventh to the thirteenth centuries AD. This sect was known from its early years for murdering its enemies and claiming these acts as a religious duty. In around 1094, Hasan-e-Sabbah refused to recognize the new Fatamid caliph (ruler) of Cairo; indeed, together with many other

Isma'ilites, Hasan-e-Sabbah found himself at odds both with successive Fatamid caliphs of Cairo, and also the 'Abbasids of Baghdad. This rift was further fueled when Hasan and his followers decided to pledge their allegiance to a deposed elder brother of the Fatamid caliph in Cairo, named Nazar—hence the appellation "Nazari Isma'ilites." It was from this time onward that the many legends surrounding this Islamic sect, who came to be known as the Hashashin, were born. The Nazari Isma'ilites practiced a form of terrorism, claiming many victims among the generals and statesmen of the 'Abbasid caliphate in what is now modern-day Iraq.

As early as 1090, Hasan and some of his followers had captured a strategic hill fortress called Alamut, near Kazvin in modern-day Iran. This hill fortress served as a power base and political center, and from here Hasan ruled as a grand master and leader of the sect, which by now had a command of a chain of strongholds all over what we know as Iraq and Iran. Hasan also commanded an unknown number of insurgents within enemy camps and cities, agents whom he sent abroad to gain information, and a whole network of propagandists whom he used as his popular mouthpiece. Two 'Abbasid caliphs fell victim to the assassins of Hasan and an attempt to recapture the stronghold of Alamut by the Seljuq sultanate failed, leaving Hasan and his followers in an even stronger position.

Extending their activities to Syria in the twelfth century, the sect seized a group of castles and strongholds in the An-Nusayriyah Mountains, the biggest prize of which was the fortress of Masyaf. From this almost impregnable fortification, the legendary and ruthless Rashid Ad-din As-sinan ruled a virtually independent assassin state, separate from the assassin headquarters at Alamut. From there he plotted several unsuccessful attempts on the life of his great enemy, the famous Ayyubid leader Saladin. It is the legends surrounding Rashid Ad-din that form the basis for the stories relating to the Old Man of the Mountains, though this name seems to have been a mistranslation of the Arabic phrase *shaykh al-jabal*, which means "mountain chief."

Many of the tales and legends associated with the assassins can be attributed to the Crusaders returning home to Europe after the third Crusade at the end of the twelfth century, but another rather surprising source seems to have been equally responsible for them: Marco Polo. At the beginning of the fourteenth century, the Venetian traveler compiled an account of the legends of the assassins, embellished with his own contributions and in his own florid style, and this account was so successful and popular that it became the model for an Arabic novel, written in 1430, which in turn was mistakenly thought to be the actual source of Marco Polo's tale. Polo's book remained the most popular source for stories about the assassins in Europe for more than 400 years.

The stories and legends of the assassins still reverberate and are deeply embedded in the psyche and culture of the Middle East and modern Arab and Islamic states. Indeed, modern politics and recent history bear witness to an assassins-versus-crusaders story being played out in the area to this day.

See also: Janus.

Helios and Poseidon

While Robert Langdon is at CERN, he and Maximilian Kohler begin discussing the organization's work. Kohler informs Langdon that the CERN scientists seek to find answers to the most basic question: where do we come from? This brings them on to the question of spirituality, with Kohler commenting that where once mankind perceived natural phenomena as the works of the gods, such as Helios and Poseidon, science can prove that such gods are "false idols."

Helios was the ancient Greek god of the sun, whose parents were either Hyperion and Theia (as mentioned in Hesiod's *Theogony*) or Hyperion and Eryphaesa (according to the Homeric *Hymn to Helios*). Whatever his parentage, Helios was the brother of Eos (the Dawn) and Selene (the Moon). One of the daughters of Helios was Circe, who in Greek mythology lured sailors to her island through the beauty of her singing. Once there, the unfortunate men were drugged and turned into swine. According to Homer's *The Odyssey*, it was only due to a warning from the god Hermes that Odysseus and his crew were able to escape a similar fate.

Helios was depicted as a young man wearing a halo and riding in a chariot. At dawn he rode his chariot out of the eastern sea and across the sky, and in the evening he descended into the west. The chariot was drawn by four horses: Pyrois, Eos, Aethon, and Phlegon. Everything that his light touched Helios was able to see, and because of his all-seeing, all-knowing abilities he was often called upon by witnesses. Probably the most famous depiction of Helios was the 100-foot-high (30.5m) statue erected on the island of Rhodes in 280 BC—which was destroyed by an earthquake around 55 years later—known to this day as the Colossus of Rhodes, one of the Seven Wonders of the ancient world.

The worship of Helios persisted up to the fourth century AD and was related to the worship of Mithra, another sun cult that at one time rivaled Christianity in popularity. Helios was even depicted in early Christian art, as in the mosaic in the necropolis beneath St Peter's Basilica on which Jesus himself is shown as Helios (the Roman equivalent being Sol Invictus).

Indeed, there has been some debate as to whether Jesus

was a follower of Helios. In their book *The Templar Revelation*, Lynn Picknett and Clive Prince cite Desmond Stewart's contention that as he was dying on the cross Jesus actually cried out, "Helios! Helios! Why has thou forsaken me?" rather than "Eli, Eli..." ("God, God..."), as quoted in Matthew's Gospel, or "Eloi, Eloi...," as stated in Mark. Picknett and Prince point out that if Jesus was actually calling out for God, he would have used the Aramaic word "Ilahi." Even some bystanders appear to have been confused by what Jesus actually said—some reputedly believed he was addressing "Elias", a reference to the prophet Elijah. Picknett and Prince argue that the association of Jesus with Helios fits in with their theory that as a savior who died and rose again, it is apt that he should emulate the daily rising and dying of the sun god.

Poseidon was one of the six original Olympians, alongside his siblings Zeus, Hades, Hestia, Demeter, and Hera. He was the god of the sea, dolphins, and horses. Noted for his changeable temperament, Poseidon could sometimes be a benevolent god, creating new lands from out of the sea, and allowing sailors to travel upon his domain freely, without obstruction. On the other hand, his bad temper was legendary, and he could cause earthquakes and violent storms if his wrath was provoked. Odysseus greatly displeased Poseidon when he blinded and then insulted Poseidon's son, Polyphemus the Cyclops. In revenge, Poseidon ensured that Odysseus's journey home was hazardous and extraordinarily lengthy, resulting in rough seas, dreadful storms, shipwrecks, and misery.

Poseidon fathered many children and was responsible for the rape of a number of women. On one occasion he even turned himself into a stallion in order to have intercourse with his sister Demeter who, in an effort to evade her brother's advances, had turned herself into a mare.

See also: CERN; Egyptian Religion; St Peter's Basilica.

Heparin

A drug used to prevent clotting, heparin is vital to many patients with thrombosis or pulmonary embolism. Discovered in 1922, and used to treat deep-vein thrombosis since the 1940s, the drug is not absorbed from the intestine, and has to be administered by injection. In *Angels & Demons* the life-saving properties of heparin are reversed, however, as it is later proven that its overuse was responsible for the murder of the Pope.

One of the main side effects of a heparin overdose is the risk of hemorrhage, i.e. excessive bleeding. If the bleeding were to occur in the brain, the effect would mimic that of a stroke and could pass as a natural death—the premise adopted in the novel.

Most patients receive heparin for only a very short period of time, usually up to seven days, during which time oral medication with drugs such as warfarin is adjusted to a maintenance dose. In the novel, it is most fortuitous for the Pope's assassin that the pontiff has been receiving daily heparin injections, thereby making it possible to administer an overdose without arousing suspicion.

See also: John Paul I, Pope.

Iambic Pentameter

When presented with a line of verse supposedly written on a folio of a secret work by Galileo, Robert Langdon recognizes it as a line of iambic pentameter. This particular style of poetry, combining five disyllabic (two-syllable) metrical "feet" in a line, reminds Langdon of Illuminati number symbolism because it combines the digits five (for the pentagram) and two (for the duality of all things).

The meter or rhythm of a line of iambic pentameter is five disyllabic feet ("iambs"), each comprising one short or unstressed syllable followed by one long or stressed syllable. For example:

"Now IS the WINter OF our DISconTENT"
from Shakespeare's *Richard III*

Examples of iambic pentameter are found in Geoffrey Chaucer's work of the fourteenth century, but it became the dominant meter of English verse from the sixteenth century onward—the most famous writer to use it being without doubt William Shakespeare. It is the pre-eminent meter in English of sonnets, blank verse, and heroic couplets; for instance, John Milton's epic poem *Paradise Lost* uses blank (unrhymed) verse in iambic pentameter.

In *Angels & Demons*, Dan Brown creates his own poem using the form, though he attributes it to the English poet John Milton:

> *From Santi's earthly tomb with demon's hole,*
> *'Cross Rome the mystic elements unfold.*
> *The path of light is laid, the sacred test,*
> *Let angels guide you on your lofty quest.*

This riddle serves as the catalyst for Langdon and Vittoria's adventures across Rome.

See also: Illuminati; Milton, John; Raphael.

Illuminati

The main plotline of *Angels & Demons* revolves around a conspiracy by the Illuminati against the Catholic Church. Clues left by artists supposedly linked to the secret organization provide the locations for the chase around the city of Rome. The culmination of the search by Robert Langdon and Vittoria Vetra comes with the discovery of the so-called Church of Illumination, concealed within a well-known landmark, Castel Sant'Angelo.

The darling subject of conspiracy theorists throughout the world, the idea of there being a group of people called the Illuminati (or "enlightened ones") is as old as the secret society itself is supposed to be. In fact, a number of disparate and nonassociated groups have called themselves by this name through recorded history. However, confusion and mystery still surround the question of whether an organization called the Illuminati actually exists today.

The first recorded use of the name came in the second century AD, when it was adopted by a group founded by a figure known as Montanus. Little is known about this former priest of the cult of Cybele, the goddess of fertility, but it is known that he converted to Christianity and soon after began his heretical movement. Eusebius, the fourth-century church historian, notes that Montanus began prophesying in the area known as Phrygia in what is now central Turkey, after having visions and entering into an ecstatic state.

This group of Illuminati included the prophetesses known as Priscilla, or Prisca, and Maximilla. The members of the group underwent frenzied religious experiences, seizures and raptures, which were regarded as messages from the Holy Spirit by the group's disciples.

Montanus was convinced that the end of the world was upon them, and tried to lay down a rigid and rigorous moral code that he saw as a way of purifying the Christian soul, in an effort to dissuade his followers from lusting after material things. Montanus and his group of Illuminati were heavily criticized by the fledgling Church of the day, which accused Montanus of failing to recognize its divinely appointed rules of law. This initial strain of Illuminati flourished in Asia Minor and North Africa until the ninth century, when it eventually died out.

The name Illuminati seems then to have lain dormant for many years, until a Spanish group calling themselves Alumbrado (which translates as Illuminati or "enlightened"), sprang up in the sixteenth century. This mystical movement claimed that once the human soul had attained a degree of perfection, it was allowed a vision of the divine and therefore could enter into direct communication with the Holy Spirit. While in this state, the devotees of the movement believed that the soul could neither advance nor regress. Therefore, it followed that strict observance of liturgy and other public observances of religious devotion were unnecessary, as true enlightenment could be received directly while in such a state. This particular group of Illuminati were persecuted mercilessly, and no fewer than three edicts were issued against them by the Inquisition, in 1568, 1574, and 1623.

In 1623, a group known as the Illumines reached France from Seville in Spain and quickly gathered a following in the Picardy region. Very little is known about this group or their doctrine. The Gurinets, a French movement formed by Pierce Guérin, a curé of Saint-Georges de Roye, in turn joined this group in 1634, before being suppressed by the Church and local authorities a year later. In 1722, a small group also called the Illumines flourished for a short time in France, but were lost from the records in around 1794.

Probably the best-known and most famous of all the historical groups to claim to be the Illuminati is the one started in Bavaria—the southern part of modern Germany—by a Freemason known as Adam Weishaupt. Weishaupt was born on February 6, 1748, at Ingolstadt, and was educated by Jesuit priests before being appointed as a professor of Natural and Canon Law at the University of Ingolstadt. This appointment was said to have been frowned upon by the local clergy, as the post had previously been in the hands of a Jesuit. It seems that Weishaupt was a young man of great intellect and the most forward-looking freethinker of his age, and while at university he quickly established a party opposed to the Jesuits. In 1777 he was invited to become a Freemason at a Lodge in Munich. Around, or possibly just before, this time, Weishaupt is said to have founded an order called the Illuminati.

It is at this point that the story becomes somewhat confused. Legend has it that a courier by the name of Lanz, working on behalf of the newly formed Illuminati, was struck by lightning and died. Revealing papers, purportedly written by Weishaupt, were found on his body, giving details of the group that Weishaupt had just formed and showing it to be an offshoot of the Masonic order. It is widely acknowledged by researchers and scholars that this story cannot be substantiated, however, and has in fact been used by anti-Masonic writers and groups associated with the Church to discredit Weishaupt and the order, claiming that its doctrines included various anti-Christian features. What remains certain, though, is that this group quickly gained popularity and status throughout Europe, becoming the foremost republican freethinkers of the time and one of the most radical offshoots of the Enlightenment. The group preferred to call themselves Perfectiblists and were still ostensibly Masonic, counting among their ranks some of the best-known Masonic members of the age. One such member, Baron Knigge, was a co-founder of the order along with Weishaupt, who managed to gain widespread recognition and popularity for the newly founded group.

At this time, Bavaria was a state dominated by conservative views and the Roman Catholic Church. In 1784, the Bavarian government banned all known secret societies, including the Illuminati and the Freemasons. This event effectively resulted in the natural collapse of the group, and the Illuminati soon floundered and faded away. Although it had been only a short-lived organization, its mark was left throughout continental Europe, as many well-known intellectuals and politicians had been members.

Thomas Jefferson, President of the United States in the early nineteenth century, commented that the Illuminati (referring to the Bavarian group) had only formed in secrecy because of "the tyranny of a despot and priests," and argued that the society had simply intended to spread knowledge and a principle of true morality. But the group had also made numerous enemies, and ironically, it is thanks to their opponents' written attacks that we know so much about the order today. *Memoirs Illustrating the History of Jacobinism*, a book published in 1797 by Abbé Augustin Barruel, contained luridly exaggerated accounts of conspiracy theories involving the Illuminati and fellow secretive organizations such as the Rosicrusians and the Knights Templar. A year later, a second book appeared, this time by John Robison, bearing the title, *Proofs of a Conspiracy Against all the Religions and Governments of Europe*. This book included large numbers of quotes from Barruel's book, reinforcing the conspiracy theories and false rumors surrounding the group. Robison claimed that there was evidence of an Illuminati conspiracy to replace all religions with humanism and all forms of rule with a one-world government. It is from these books that much of the speculation and false reports about the group originates, something that has persisted over time to the present day.

Some modern-day researchers claim that the Bavarian Illuminati lives on, infiltrating organizations and political movements to try and bring about its avowed aim of a single world government, or New World Order as it is sometimes known. The Yale Skull and Bones Society—the elite club of which many a US president has been a member, including in more modern times George Bush Senior and George W. Bush—is claimed to be a hotbed of Illuminati machinations and intrigue; some also claim that the nongovernmental organizations and think tanks known as the Bilderberg Group, Trilateral Commission, and Council on Foreign Relations are also fronts for the Illuminati. It is said that the Illuminati ultimately want to rule the world, using such tactics as financial control of markets and banks, manipulation of foreign policy and conflicts, assassinations, terrorism, and many other methods.

The question remains: does a group known as the Illuminati exist today, plotting world domination and one-world government? The idea of a secret society determined to rule the world readily appeals to many conspiracy theorists, who often seem to need a single faceless group to blame for all the world's ills and problems. This isn't to say that there are not groups around whose aim is to form a New World Order, but the evidence of an actual Illuminati, plotting and planning the next coup, conflict, assassination, or market collapse, is scant and difficult to prove.

In recent times the legendary status of the Illuminati has been a notable feature of cultural iconography. British author David Icke claims that the Illuminati are a race of alien beings who control many of the world's governments, major businesses, banks, and royalty. The Illuminati also emerges from time to time in the sphere of popular culture—in the 2001 movie *Lara Croft: Tomb Raider*, for example, a group of baddies calling themselves the Illuminati hatch a plan to rule the world.

Sadly for fans of *Angels & Demons* there is no direct evidence to suggest that Dan Brown's version of the origins of a group called the Illuminati can be traced to sixteenth-century Rome. Similarly, Brown's assertion of Galileo's involvement with this organization and the Church's "purging" of four so-called Illuminati scientists in 1668 is also doubtful. This, along with the idea of a Path of

Illumination and the Illuminati Diamond, all seem to be ingenious creations emanating from Brown's fantastic imagination.

See also: Freemasonry; Galileo Galilei; Knights Templar; New World Order.

Isola Tiberina

The Isola Tiberina is an island on the River Tiber in Rome, and the site of Robert Langdon's miraculous recovery after his death-defying fall from the helicopter.

Uninhabited for much of its history, Isola Tiberina was first settled around the sixth century BC, so legend has it, by abandoned slaves who had become too weak to work. On the island, the slaves are said to have begun to worship the Greek deity Asclepius, the god of healing, and the island has been associated with healing and hospitals ever since. A strange legend grew up around the island, to the effect that when the Romans took the statue of the god Asclepius from its sanctuary at Kos in Greece, in 293 BC, they dragged it up the River Tiber, but upon entering the region of the Isola, the god appeared as a snake and slithered onto the island. The Romans, seeing this as a sign that the god wanted his sanctuary there, decided to encase the island in marble, building the walls in the shape of a boat, which is the shape the island appears to have today. Some traces of the original decoration on the southeast side of the island are still visible, with a carving of a serpent particularly prominent.

The Romans eventually built a large temple to Asclepius on the island itself, said to be where the sick could wait for the healing god to visit them in their dreams, in the hope that he would bring a cure with him. Today archeological remains have been found indicating that votive offerings were made to the god here. These included statuettes of arms, legs, heads, and other body parts, which were offered as thanks.

Also on the island is the small tenth-century church of San Bartolomeo, which has been flooded and rebuilt a number of times. This church is a fantastic mixture of architectural styles, encompassing the Romanesque, the Baroque, and twentieth-century materials.

In AD 154, a group of Fatebenefratelli monks established a hospital on the island, the location no doubt chosen as a result of its symbolism and earlier reputation. This site is still occupied by a hospital today and is considered to be the most fashionable place to give birth in Rome, with the look of a sanctuary on the outside and the feel of a church on the inside.

See also: Rome.

Janus

The Roman god of doors and gates, beginnings and endings, Janus was represented as a double-faced head, with each face looking in opposite directions (though occasionally he was depicted as four-faced on some coins, and at times with either a single or double beard). In modern times this depiction has led to Janus becoming a codeword for a two-faced or duplicitous person, as demonstrated by the character responsible for directing the activities of the Hassassin, who adopts this alias in *Angels & Demons*.

It is thought that the worship of Janus goes back to the time of Romulus, or even before the founding of Rome. Janus was invoked first out of all the gods in the regular liturgies of the time. January, the first month of the modern calendar—and the eleventh month of the Roman calendar—is named after him. His festival took place on the ninth of this month, known as the Agonium; the beginning of the day, month, and year were sacred to him.

Janus was associated with marriages and births—situations associated with new beginnings—and he seems to represent the transitional aspect of countryside and cities, ancient and modern, primitive and civilized. Legend states that Janus is ready to intervene when needed at times of war on behalf of Rome and his temple gates would be kept open when conflict ensued; in peacetime they would be closed.

The most famous temple to Janus was on the Forum Olitorium in Rome. He also had a portal dedicated to him on the Forum Romanum, through which the Roman legionaries went to war. Much superstition was attached to these gates, however, and there was a correct way and an incorrect way to march through them.

Janus was said to have married Queen Camese of Latium with whom he shared the kingdom. The legend goes that it was one of their children, Tiberinius, who gave his name to the River Tiber that flows through Rome.

See also: Hassassin; Rome.

John Paul I, Pope

After Robert Langdon has digested the news that the Pope has been murdered, he reflects on media speculation about the sudden death of a previous pontiff, Pope John Paul I, after only 33 days in office.

Albino Luciani was born near Belluno, Italy, on October 17, 1912, into an obscure family. He rose through the ranks of the Church on merit, becoming patriarch of Venice and a cardinal. Pope Paul VI, his predecessor, had reformed the conclave that elects the new Pope, depriving those more than 80 years of age of their vote, insisting that balloting must be secret, and massively increasing the membership. Although many more non-Italians were serving as cardinals at the time, on August 26, 1978—the first day of the conclave—Cardinal Luciani was elected and became Pope John Paul I, thereby maintaining Italy's hold on the papacy.

John Paul I refused to be crowned at first, emphasizing his humility by accepting only the woolen pallium—a ceremonial garment that encircles the shoulders—which all Roman Catholic archbishops are entitled to wear. He saw himself more as a shepherd watching over his flock than as a prince.

Among his other departures from the norm, the new Pope chose a double name, honoring his two predecessors by doing so. Here was a man who would make changes to the church, it seemed. However, on September 28, 1978, after a pontificate which had lasted a mere month and three days, a heart attack killed him. There was much wild speculation at the time that the Pope had been poisoned—speculation fanned at least in part by the fact that more conservative elements in the Church had been wondering what radical changes this unorthodox but increasingly admired pontiff might introduce in the future. The subject has been discussed by David Yallop in his book *In God's Name*, in which the suggestion is made that John Paul I had been murdered and the Vatican had attempted a cover-up.

John Cornwell outlined an alternative theory—that the Pope died of a pulmonary embolism—in *A Thief in the Night*. There is even reference to the assassination of a Pope John Paul I in the film *The Godfather: Part III*, indicating how widespread suspicion had become that the death had been unnatural.

John Paul I published several letters, collectively entitled *Illustrissimi*, which were addressed to authors and fictional characters, giving an insight into his personal views. The current pontiff, Pope John Paul II, honored his memory by choosing the same double names as his predecessor.

See also: Celestine V, Pope; Vatican, The.

Knights Templar

When Robert Langdon and the Camerlengo are considering the threat posed to the Church by the apparent revival of the Illuminati in *Angels & Demons*, Langdon reflects on other organizations that the Church has been accused of persecuting over the centuries, including the Knights Templar. The order was active in the Holy Land at the same time as the Hassassin, a group that casts a long shadow over the novel.

In 1118, Hughes de Payens of Champagne and eight fellow knights came together in Jerusalem before the Patriarch, or ruler, to make a vow to become the Poor Knights of Christ, subsisting on charity. Shortly afterward they began to dress in white habits, similar to those worn by

Cistercian monks, but with the addition of a red cross. The founder of the Cistercians, Bernard of Clairvaux (who was later made a saint), used his huge influence to further their cause. Their declared mission at that time was to defend the roads carrying Christian pilgrims to the Holy Land. These travelers, who increased in number soon after the First Crusade (1096–9), believed that by performing the journey their souls would find favor with God in Heaven.

The Roman Catholic Church welcomed the protection the knights afforded to these pious Christians. Since their work involved defending the Temple Mount in Jerusalem, they became known as Knights Templar and, with the increase in their influence and power, many knights from across Europe rallied to their banner. In modern-day terms they saw this employment as a career opportunity, despite having taken vows of chastity and austerity.

Since their purpose was considered laudable, favors were granted to the knights to support them in their holy work. Exemption from taxes and tithes helped to swell their coffers, and grants of land and property further enriched them. Other benefits they enjoyed included having total control over their own affairs and independence from lay authority. Throughout different countries they erected castles as bases for their military campaigns, and chapels within the secular structures to serve their spiritual needs. They were, after all, soldiers of Christ—or so they claimed. It was believed that Temple Mount had been the site of King Solomon's temple and in consequence Templar castles were designed to resemble this fabled building.

Inevitably their status led to feelings of jealousy among other followers of Christ. Rulers of countries also began to envy the Templars, and perhaps to fear this independent power within their own realms. The ruthless Philip IV of France arrested large numbers of Knights Templar in 1307, torturing and executing many. Some were forced under duress to admit heresy and other dreadful crimes, leading

Pope Clement V—another Frenchman under the influence of Philip—to dissolve the order. Their wealth and property found receptive new owners.

The downfall of the Templars was a direct consequence of their own success. It is hard to tell whether their secret rituals were blasphemous, as their enemies claimed. It is likely, however, that some members broke their oaths of poverty, and certainly over the two centuries of their existence the Poor Knights of Christ had become extremely rich. Any organization attaining massive wealth and influence is a target for envy from the less successful. The Templars' big mistake, perhaps, was in not cultivating sufficiently strong allies and in alienating some who might have lent them assistance. Their organization was a phenomenon of the twelfth and thirteenth centuries that still holds a strong fascination today.

Studies on the history of the Knights Templar has led to assertions that a refugee band of Templars, who imparted secret information to the early Masons in Scotland, were partially responsible for the origins of the Freemasons. However, there is a lack of adequate accurate historical evidence to back up this link, and so the connection between the two organizations remains tenuous.

See also: Freemasonry; Illuminati.

Langdon, Robert

Dan Brown employs Robert Langdon as the lead character in both *Angels & Demons* and his other worldwide bestseller, *The Da Vinci Code*; he is also expected to appear again in a third adventure. Langdon is described as a Harvard professor who lectures in Religious Symbology, and is said to be the author of more than a dozen books. (In reality there is no such post at Harvard, although two genuine Harvard professors—Nicolas P. Constas, whose field is icons and iconography in religion, and Kimberley C. Patton, whose areas are funerary cults, dream interpretation, and the iconography of sacrifice—are indeed involved in the kind of work in which Robert Langdon is supposed to be an expert.

One of the major elements in the plot of *Angels & Demons* is the unconventional use of ambigrams as brands on the unfortunate cardinals chosen by the Hassassin. In his acknowledgments Dan Brown pays tribute to the artist John Langdon who designed the ambigrams used in the book. This suggests that the character's name is drawn from that of the artist, who published a book in 1992 called *Wordplay*, featuring various ambigrams and commentary about the words used.

The fictitious Robert Langdon has a real website: www.robertlangdon.com.

See also: Ambigrams; Hassassin.

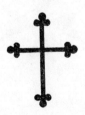

Lucifer

In *Angels & Demons*, Robert Langdon makes reference to the Church's assertion that Lucifer was another name for the Devil. However, he informs Kohler that the Illuminati perceived Lucifer as the "bringer of light," which is the literal meaning of the word, from the Latin *lux*, meaning light, and *fero*, meaning carry or bring.

"Lucifer" is the Latin name for the planet Venus, the brightest morning star. In Hebrew texts Lucifer is referred to as the "shining one," also relating to Venus. The association of Lucifer with the Devil comes about because of certain passages in the Bible, which somewhat tenuously link Satan with the coming of light:

> *He replied, "I watched how Satan fell, like lightning out of the sky."* (Luke 10:18)

> *Then the fifth angel blew the trumpet; and I saw a star that had fallen from heaven to earth . . .* (Revelation 9:1)

Rather than signifying the bringer of light, in Christian tradition the term "Lucifer" has become the name of the principal fallen angel who was once as bright as the morning star, although according to this tradition the word "Lucifer" is not actually the name of the Devil, but only a description of his fallen condition. Perversely, some editions of the Bible, notably the King James version, use the word "Lucifer" as a proper name rather than as a descriptive term, which it really should be. Thus, Isaiah 14:12 reads: "How art thou fallen from heaven, O Lucifer, son of the morning! How art thou cut down to the ground, which didst weaken the nations!"

However, this quote from the Book of Isaiah actually relates to the fall of the King of Babylon, which has been misinterpreted by successive Christian commentators as the fall of the rebel angel Satan from heaven, and hence links the words "Satan" and "Lucifer" together to mean the same entity. Even so, as the King of Babylon is being addressed in this instance, the phrase cannot possibly be intended to mean Satan. In fact, the Hebrew versions of this passage use the word *eill* to represent Lucifer, meaning "howl." The confusion of this term and the description "shining one" probably arose from a mistranslation from Hebrew to Greek by a copyist who translated *eill* as *ell* (*eospearos* in Greek), meaning "shining one." Jerome subsequently translated this in the fifth century AD from the Greek into the Latin as the name Lucifer, a mistake that was perpetuated by the King James Bible in the seventeenth century. And so the confusion over the name Lucifer has continued throughout the Christian era.

Interestingly, scholars have pointed out that in Revelation 22:16 Jesus supposedly gives himself the title "bright star of the dawn," and certainly in this instance Jesus has never been confused with Satan as Lucifer has been.

See also: Shaitan.

Matthew 16:18

At one dramatic point in the novel, Camerlengo Ventresca races down the main aisle inside St Peter's Basilica, shouting the words, "Upon this rock I will build my church," a quote from Matthew 16:18. As he enters the Niche of the Palliums, Ventresca tells Robert Langdon that he knows where the antimatter is hidden. It is at this moment that Langdon realizes what the camerlengo meant by quoting those words: he was referring to the tomb of St Peter, upon which, quite literally, the basilica was built.

The complete quote in the Bible, attributed to Jesus himself speaking to Simon Peter, reads: "And I say also unto thee, That thou art Peter, and upon this rock I will build my church; and the gates of hell shall not prevail against it." (In Greek, the name Peter is Petros, meaning "stone.")

The meaning of the words has engendered a great deal of debate among scholars, which centers around four main arguments:

- It is probable that Jesus did not intend to found an autonomous Church at all.
- The words relate to the resurrection, and not to the foundation of a separate sect.
- The quote should be seen in the context of Jesus's death, when Peter denied him three times, and also relates to a quote within Luke (22:32), which states that Peter "must lend strength to your brothers."
- The reference should be interpreted simply as a promise and a blessing.

The authenticity of the quote has also been called into question. Only Matthew's Gospel places the naming of Peter here, some time into Jesus's ministry, by which time the apostles are already well established. In John 1:42, the name is conferred to the disciple at his first meeting with Jesus, and from that moment on he is referred to as Simon Peter. Mark 3:16 mentions the naming of Peter shortly after the appointment of the twelve apostles.

There are two main interpretations of the significance of Peter's name. Firstly, that the term relates to Peter's unremitting belief in Jesus being the Messiah, which was evident long before Jesus's confession to the apostles that he was indeed the Messiah. According to this argument, the most significant factor about Peter's name is the confession of faith, both from Peter and Jesus, and it is upon this faith that the Christian Church was to be built.

The second interpretation, and probably the easiest to understand, is that Peter himself was the "rock" on which Christianity would be founded—especially since Jesus was addressing Peter personally. This quote has been likened to Isaiah 2:1, which states: "God said, 'Behold, I have found a rock on which I can build and base the world.' Therefore he called Abraham a rock."

Considering Jesus's in-depth knowledge of the Scriptures, it is highly likely that he was conversant with this passage and understood the implications of his words to Peter. There is no doubt that elsewhere the Gospels place a special importance upon Peter, as Matthew 16:18 appears to, although it is still debatable whether the renaming of Peter should be attributed to Jesus or to the Gospels' authors.

See also: Peter, St; St Peter's Basilica; Vatican, The.

Michelangelo

The life of the great Renaissance artist Michelangelo Buonarroti began in the small Tuscan town of Caprese, Italy, in 1475, but his family soon moved to Florence, which he always regarded as his home. At the age of 13 he became an apprentice to the artist Domenico Ghirlandaio—it is thought against the wishes of his father. As a significant contributor to the art of the Vatican, major scenes in *Angels & Demons* are played out beneath Michelangelo's magnificent frescoes. (Some sources also claim that he designed the uniforms of the Vatican Swiss Guard, although this is generally accepted not to have been the case.)

After a year of work with Ghirlandaio, Michelangelo left to study the classical sculptures in the gardens of the wealthy and influential Florentine family, the Medicis; indeed, he always considered himself first and foremost a sculptor. During his time at the Medici home he met two members of the family who were to become the future Popes Leo X and Clement VII. To develop his understanding of anatomy he used corpses for study, a practice disapproved of by the Church, but it is believed he carved a wooden crucifix for the Church of Santo Spirito as recompense.

During the 1490s, there was political unrest in Florence, and in 1494 the Medici family were overthrown, leading Michelangelo to migrate to Rome, where he once more studied classical works. Between 1496 and 1498 he sculpted Bacchus, one of only a few pagan subjects that he produced. The *Pietà* now standing in St Peter's, Rome, is a marble statue of the Virgin mourning the dead Christ, and was carved between 1498 and 1499; it is a magnificent work, showing great understanding of a difficult composition. On his return to Florence, Michelangelo carved possibly his most famous work, *David*, an athletic and powerful figure, the embodiment of the Renaissance ideal.

In 1508 Michelangelo was summoned to Rome by Pope Julius II, who commissioned him to work on his tomb and the ceiling of the Sistine Chapel. Julius was a considerable patron of the arts; at the same time Raphael was decorating the Vatican Stanze. Michelangelo was reluctant to undertake the painting, but was given no choice, so he discussed plans for a depiction of the twelve apostles with the Pope. As the work progressed over the next four years, Michelangelo—working mostly alone—evolved a design that incorporates over 400 figures. Scenes from the Book of Genesis include the creation of Adam, the temptation and fall of Adam and

Eve, and stories of Noah. Michelangelo also includes 40 generations of the ancestors of Christ, starting with Abraham. Upon completion of the ceiling, Michelangelo began work on the tomb, carving a statue of Moses, but after the death of Julius, plans were scaled down considerably.

The accession of a Medici pontiff, Pope Leo X, led to Michelangelo working back in Florence on projects such as the Medici Chapel, for the benefit of the Medici family rather than the papacy in general. The figures of Dawn, Day, Dusk, and Night are among his most famous sculptures, and they represent the inevitable cycles that include life and death. In 1534 he returned to Rome, where he was to spend the rest of his life, taking on ever more spectacular commissions.

The Last Judgment, which decorates one wall of the Sistine Chapel, is the largest fresco of the sixteenth century. Completed in 1541, it shows Christ separating mankind into the saved, who ascend to Heaven, and the damned, who are depicted on their descent into Hell. Controversy over the portrayal of nudes in the chapel was voiced at the time, notably by the papal master of ceremonies Biagio da Cesena, who then found himself depicted in the portion of Hell. Michelangelo included himself as the flayed skin of St Bartholomew. Later sensibilities did lead to another artist being commissioned to add drapery to the figures after Michelangelo's death.

From 1546 Michelangelo worked as an architect on St Peter's Basilica, amending plans left by some of his predecessors and designing the dome. Around the base he created a columned walkway, the columns acting to support the dome.

He died in 1564, and his body was taken back to Florence and buried in the Church of Santa Croce.

See also: Raphael; St Peter's Basilica; Sistine Chapel; Swiss Guard; Vatican, The.

Milton, John

In *Angels & Demons*, this great English poet is said to have written the verse that will solve the mystery of the location of the Illuminati lair. As a radical Protestant during the unrest of the English Civil War, Milton was a strong critic of the Catholic Church, but he was also a devoutly religious man, and so it would have been highly unlikely that in reality he would have been involved in any anti-religious secret societies, such as the Illuminati. However, he was also a vigorous proponent of free speech (he once asserted that, "Who kills a man kills a reasonable creature; but he who destroys a book destroys reason itself"), so it is unlikely he would have objected to his name being used in a modern work of fiction.

The family into which Milton was born in 1608 was Protestant, and his father seems to have encouraged his son in his early writing. The young John was educated at St Paul's in London and then at Cambridge University, at Christ's College. He had been writing poetry since the age of nine, and refined this skill at Cambridge, composing a number of poems, including, "Ode on the Morning of Christ's Nativity." This was written in English, although Latin was the more common language for poetry among the university elite.

After leaving university, Milton retired to the country for five years, reading history and philosophy, in what was to be the foundation for his liberal ideas. In 1638 he embarked on a trip to Italy, where he traveled to Rome, Florence, and Naples, and met many scholars. Significantly he also made a visit to the aged Galileo, still under house arrest after his condemnation by the Inquisition for heresy. The artist Annibale Gatti later envisaged this meeting, painting the two men in conversation. Dan Brown uses the historic encounter as the basis for his fictional plot device of Milton writing a secret verse on a folio of a work by Galileo.

Milton returned home to England in 1639 to find that

the political situation between King Charles I and Parliament had deteriorated dramatically. Despite plans to write an epic Arthurian poem, Milton spent most of the period between 1641 and 1660 writing pamphlets, as an ardent supporter of the Parliamentarian cause. He also wrote on the subject of divorce in his *The Doctrine and Discipline of Divorce*—his own unhappy marriage to a much younger woman doubtless influencing his thoughts. In 1644 Milton published the pamphlet *Areopagitica*, his defense of the freedom of the press and plea for civil liberties. He refers to his meeting with Galileo, and was clearly motivated by the censorship of Galileo's work.

In the aftermath of the execution of the King, Milton wrote a defense of the right of the people to depose or execute a tyrant. This was to prove dangerous—the monarchy was restored in 1660 and a warrant was issued for the poet's arrest. Milton was fortunate to have supporters who defended him against the reprisals perpetrated on some of the regicides, and there may have been some sympathy for his position, since he had become blind over time. He was allowed to live in retirement, and he reverted to his poetical work.

Milton is best remembered for his masterpiece, the epic poem *Paradise Lost*, first published in 1667. Written in blank (i.e. unrhymed) verse in iambic pentameters, and originally published in ten books, it tells the story of Satan's expulsion from Heaven, and the temptation and fall of Adam and Eve. From his description of the universe it is clear that Milton understood the Copernican theory—he may even have discussed it with Galileo—but he chose to use the accepted geocentric Ptolemaic model that kept the earth and man at the center of the universe. An impoverished Milton sold the copyright in *Paradise Lost* for five pounds, with an additional five pounds to follow depending on sales. In the sequel, *Paradise Regained*, Christ redeems the errors of Adam and overcomes Satan in the wilderness; it was published along with *Samson Agonistes* in 1671.

In later life, Milton found an amiable companion in his third wife and he moved to the English countryside—Chalfont St Giles in Buckinghamshire—after an outbreak of the plague in London in 1665.

After his death in 1674, Milton was buried at the Church of St Giles, Cripplegate, in London, next to the father who had encouraged him and whose support he had recognized in his work "Ad Patrem", or "To Father."

See also: Copernicus, Nicolaus; Galileo Galilei; Gatti, Annibale; Iambic Pentameter.

Nazca Lines

Having flown in to Rome's Leonardo da Vinci airport from Geneva, Robert Langdon and Vittoria Vetra wait for transport to take them to Vatican City. Hearing the whirring of a helicopter, Langdon becomes nervous when he realizes that this is to be their mode of transportation. He muses that the last time he had the pleasure of a helicopter ride was to look at the Nazca lines drawn on the Andean Palpa Valley in Peru.

These lines were believed to have been created by the Nazca people, who lived in the region around 200 BC–AD 600. Sometimes described as "geoglyphs," the lines cover approximately 400 square miles (1,040sq km) of dry, stony desert known as the Pampa Colorado. Their creators formed the lines by clearing away the red stones and soil on the surface, to reveal the lighter subsoil. Some geoglyphs—

mainly the anthropomorphic figures—are found on the hill slopes that edge the desert. In total there are more than 300 geoglyphs, comprising geometric shapes, animal designs, plants, and figures, including whales, birds, lizards, a tree, hands, a flower, a triangle, spirals, a star, and what some have described as an astronaut. Other designs appear to be completely arbitrary, as is the positioning of the geoglyphs, which invariably overlap each other. Even so, the Nazca designs do have defined entrances, suggesting that people walked along the lines, perhaps as part of a religious ceremony.

The enigma surrounding the dating and hence production of the lines has led to a number of conjectures to explain who created them and why. These range from the belief that they are alien landing strips, proposed by Eric von Däniken (who also suggested that many of the designs were actually created by the people of the area in an effort to persuade the aliens to return), to the astronomical-calendar theory, put forward by the German archeologist and mathematician Maria Reiche. She argued that the geoglyphs point in the direction of important stars, planets, and celestial events. The problem with this idea, however, is that over time the direction of the stars and planets have altered, so unless a date is known for the construction of the lines, it cannot be stated categorically where the lines were pointing. Other researchers have put forward different notions: Robert Bast suggests the lines commemorated the great flood, while Gilbert de Jong believes they represented a Nazcan zodiac. Markus Reindel suggests they marked underground water supplies, whereas Professor Helaine Siverman attests that the figures represented clan signs of the different peoples in the region.

Unfortunately, the Nazca lines are now showing signs of erosion and destruction, partly due to human interference in the search for artifacts, but also because of construction work and tracks that run through the site.

New World Order

In *Angels & Demons*, the apparently resurrected Illuminati are portrayed as an organization hell-bent on establishing a New World Order. At one point during a discussion of the mysterious sect, Robert Langdon tells Vittoria Vetra about some of the symbolism on the American one-dollar bill, specifically the design incorporating the pyramid and the motto of "New Secular Order," translated from the Latin *Novus Ordo Seclorum*. Certainly the idea behind the New World Order is another tantalizing concept for conspiracy theorists and writers of a paranoid disposition to explore. But what exactly is it? And does such a conspiracy really exist?

The theory goes something like this. The New World Order (or NWO) is a world management system, designed to enslave and control populations under a single world government and currency system. Under this system, those behind the NWO would seek to curtail dramatically personal freedoms, individual rights and responsibilities, freedom of speech, national sovereignty, constitutional government, religious freedoms, private property and business, and even personality development.

There are those who believe the European Union model is a part of this conspiracy; others argue the Council on Foreign Relations and other influential think tanks like the Bilderberg Group and the Trilateral Commission are part of the bigger picture. Conspiracy theorists believe that the NWO is to be found everywhere in society, permeating through and influencing all strata of government, business, and finance.

The idea that a single faceless organization is plotting world domination and control is not a new one. Many philosophers and intellectuals have believed that such a model is a legitimate and worthy aim, and have set up secret societies and organizations dedicated to achieving exactly this outcome. However, most operate on a small and inconsequential scale, never managing to become the global force that such ambitious aims require.

Even former US president Abraham Lincoln seems to have believed that there were higher powers conspiring against him. He was once quoted as saying:

> The money powers prey upon the nation in times of peace and conspire against it in times of adversity. It is more despotic than a monarchy, more insolent than autocracy, and more selfish than bureaucracy. It denounces as public enemies all who question its methods or throw light upon its crimes. I have two great enemies, the Southern Army in front of me and the Bankers in the rear. Of the two, the one at my rear is my greatest foe . . . corporations have been enthroned and an era of corruption in high places will follow, and the money powers of the country will endeavor to prolong its reign by working upon the prejudices of the people until the wealth is aggregated in the hands of a few, and the Republic is destroyed.

The term "New World Order" has come to serve as a blanket phrase to cover many things, including secret societies and cabals, government manipulation and control (Big Brother *is* watching you), banking and financial organizations, family bloodlines, royal houses, policy-influencing groups, and just about everything in between. The problem is, if we look at the idea of a NWO in these terms then the theory in conspiracy theory actually becomes fact—these organizations do actually exist, governments do manipulate and control, and financial houses are so powerful that they can topple regimes and nations (think of the power that the World Bank holds).

All of this falls neatly into the box-within-a-box theory—i.e. what we think of as our cogent, logical, ostensibly free world is just the inner box in a Russian-doll-like system, housed within a bigger, unseen box that actually controls everything. In order for the NWO to become all-encompassing, its talons of influence need to be both far-reaching and completely untraceable. For instance, the theory goes that members of secret societies such as the Templars and the Masons will carry out the work of the NWO without knowing it—only the upper echelons and a few individuals will be aware of the greater plan.

Certain religious groups and millennial cults believe that the NWO is a Satanist plot, cooked up by devil-worshiping families, and that this is a struggle that has taken place over the past 2,000 years at least; many point to the Book of Revelation in the New Testament as a prophecy of things to come. In the United States, militias and small groups of individuals have taken to organizing themselves against what they see as interference in their individual freedoms. Sometimes these groups have faced the wrath of the federal government, with tragic results in the cases of the massacres at Waco and Ruby Ridge.

But what is the ultimate aim of the NWO? When every nongovernmental organization (NGO) is in its control, when every major religious movement is subservient to its wishes, when it has infiltrated every financial house, national government, intelligence group, and political movement—what then? What comes after world domination? According to many conspiracy theorists, we may soon find out . . .

See also: Armageddon; Dollar-Bill Symbolism; Freemasonry; Illuminati.

Obelisks

In *Angels & Demons*, Robert Langdon realizes that certain ancient Egyptian obelisks located in Rome are pointers to the site of the next murder of a cardinal, and ultimately to the mysterious Church of the Illuminati. These obelisks stand outside the Church of Santa Maria del Popolo, within St Peter's Square, outside the Church of Santa Maria della Vittoria in the Piazza Barberini (since removed), and at the Piazza Navona. There is also an obelisk in the Piazza della Rotunda outside the Pantheon, although Robert and Vittoria soon realize this does not indicate one of the locations they are seeking.

Closely associated with the ancient Egyptian cult of the sun, an obelisk (Egyptian name *tekhen*) is a long, thin, four-sided stone monument that tapers to a pyramid-shaped top. Its shape was representative of the first ray of light at the Creation. To underline this, the ancient Egyptians sheathed the pyramid tip in gold foil to reflect the sun, although according to their inscriptions two obelisks erected by the female pharaoh Hatshepsut (1479–1425 BC) were completely covered in gold foil.

Although usually erected within temples, there are some examples of smaller obelisks raised outside private tombs in Egypt. From the New Kingdom (1550–1069 BC) onward, obelisks were often erected in pairs in front of temple pylons, the monumental entrances to the temples. They were carved with hieroglyphs that provided details about the pharaoh responsible for their erection. The base of an obelisk often depicted baboons giving praise to the morning sun as it rose above them, a recognition of the obelisk's connection with the sun cult.

The ancient Egyptians believed that cult objects were

imbued with a life of their own and, as such, obelisks were given names and offerings were made to them. Their importance was underlined by the tremendous technological thought and physical effort that went into the cutting, preparation, transportation, and erection of these massive monuments. Usually carved from granite, some are over 98 feet (29.9m) tall and weigh over 450 tonnes. At Hatshepsut's mortuary temple at Deir el-Bahri a wall painting illustrates the transportation of two obelisks. These lie base to base on a large barge that is being pulled by 27 boats rowed by 850 men.

During the Ptolemaic (305–30 BC) and Roman (30 BC–AD 395) periods, the Romans removed many obelisks from Egypt, and today there are now more ancient obelisks in Rome—thirteen in total—than anywhere else in the world. The largest obelisk in Rome is situated in the Piazza San Giovanni. It had originally been erected in the temple of Karnak by the pharaoh Thutmose III (1479–1425 BC), but in AD 326 the Christian Roman Emperor Constantine the Great removed it. By the time of his death in AD 337, however, it had only got as far as Alexandria in northern Egypt. It was finally left up to his son to transport the 400-tonne obelisk to Rome.

Other examples of obelisks in Europe are Cleopatra's Needle in London from Heliopolis, and the obelisk at the Place de Concorde, Paris, which had originally been set up in the temple at Luxor.

The five obelisks referred to in *Angels & Demons* are all real. The one in the Piazza della Rotunda in front of the Pantheon was once part of a pair, erected at the Ra temple in Heliopolis by the pharaoh Rameses II. When brought to Rome it originally stood in the temple of Isis, but by the fourteenth century it was on the Capitoline Hill. In 1711, Pope Clement XI arranged for its transfer to the Piazza della Rotunda, and a fountain was incorporated at the base.

The obelisk that points the way to the first cardinal's

murder can be found at the Piazza del Popolo, outside the church containing the Chigi Chapel. Originally standing at Heliopolis in Egypt, it was erected by two pharaohs: Seti I, who carved three sides, and his son Rameses II, who dedicated the fourth side. It is 78 feet (23.8m) high and weighs around 235 tonnes, so when Emperor Augustus decided to remove it to Rome in 100 BC, he was undertaking a massive task. He placed the obelisk in the Circus Maximus in Rome, but it eventually toppled over, and was not re-erected until Pope Sixtus V made it the centerpiece of the Piazza del Popolo in 1589. Further developments in the piazza saw the lion sculptures that now surround the obelisk added between 1816 and 1824.

The second cardinal's murder in the novel occurs at the base of the obelisk in St Peter's Square. The Vatican obelisk is unusual in that it is not covered in the customary hieroglyphs—whether by design or otherwise it is now impossible to say. It may date from the reign of Pharaoh Amenenhat II and be from Heliopolis, or from the rule in Egypt of Emperor Augustus and come from Alexandria. This obelisk, which is even larger than its Piazza del Popolo cousin at 82 feet (25m) high and 320 tonnes, was moved to Rome by Caligula in AD 37. It was erected in the Caligula Circus (which subsequently became the Vatican Circus), occupying a site to the side of the current St Peter's Basilica. As part of the regeneration of the basilica and its square, Pope Sixtus V arranged to have the monument relocated in 1586. This particular obelisk had never fallen or been pulled down. Egyptologist Labib Habachi offers an explanation for this in his book *The Obelisk of Egypt*:

> In the Vatican Circus innumerable Christians, including St Peter, were put to death, and the reason this obelisk was not later overturned as were all the others in Rome was that it was looked upon as the last witness to the martyrdom of St Peter.

Dan Brown places the site of the third cardinal's murder, the Church of Santa Maria della Vittoria, on the Piazza Barberini, although it is actually on Via XX Settembre. Robert Langdon suggests that the obelisk that stood in this square had been recently moved due to construction work that may have damaged it, but this was not so in reality. The history of the obelisk is not well recorded, but it was possibly created in Egypt in the second century for the Emperor Hadrian, and has had several locations since its arrival in Rome. It was moved from the Piazza Barberini in 1822 by Pope Pius VII to its present home in the Pincio Gardens.

The last of the captured cardinals is drowned in the waters of the *Fountain of the Four Rivers* in the Piazza Navona. The fountain and the square in which it sits are dominated by the obelisk that the Roman emperor Domitian had carved from red granite at Aswan in Egypt. It is decorated with images of a goddess presenting Domitian with the double crowns of Upper and Lower Egypt, which he is receiving in the manner of a pharaoh. Probably created around AD 81, at the time of Domitian's accession, it was transported to Rome to stand between the temples of Serapis and Isis. In the early fourth century, Maxentius moved it to the Circus de Massenzio, where it toppled over and broke.

As the *Fountain of the Four Rivers* was planned by Bernini on behalf of Pope Innocent X, the obelisk was reclaimed and placed in the center of the fountain with a dove added to the top, the family symbol of the Pope's Pamphili family. It has dominated the Piazza Navona since 1651.

See also: Bernini, Gian Lorenzo; Chigi Chapel; Fountain of the Four Rivers; Pantheon, The; Santa Maria del Popolo; Santa Maria della Vittoria; Vatican, The.

Oculus

The Pantheon in Rome has an opening at the top of its dome known as the "oculus." The name derives from the Latin for "eye," and is usually used to describe a small round window, though in this case the diameter of the hole is 29 feet (8.8m).

Originally built by the Roman general Agrippa in 27 BC, and dedicated to all the pagan gods of Rome, the Pantheon was completely reconstructed by Hadrian in AD 120–24. The oculus in the center of the tall dome provides the only source of natural light into the building. Pope Boniface IV was given the structure in 609, when it became the first pagan temple to be converted into a Christian church. As part of the purification process the Pope had 28 cartloads of the bones of martyrs brought to the place now known as the Church of Santa Maria ad Martyres, and had them buried beneath the altar. There is a legend that as hymns were sung the assembled Romans saw a swarm of devils rise up to fly out of the hole in the dome. Understandably, therefore, Langdon and Vittoria make a connection between the oculus and the "demon's hole" mentioned in the cryptic poem they are trying to decipher, but it turns out to be a red herring.

See also: Pantheon, The; Rome.

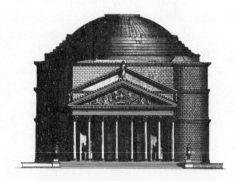

Pantheon, The

Robert Langdon and Vittoria Vetra initially head to the Pantheon in search of the "first altar of science" and the tomb of Santi, more commonly known as Raphael. It is there that they suppose the first cardinal will be murdered, although they find it hard to believe that such a savage act could be carried out in full view of hundreds of tourists, especially in a monument that has only one escape route. Indeed, it proves to be a red herring.

The Pantheon is one of the most impressive ancient monuments that survive in Rome, and certainly the most complete. Michelangelo described it as being of "angelic and not human design." Although now known as the Roman Catholic Church of Santa Maria ad Martyres, it was formerly a temple built to honor all the Roman gods. However, in spite of Langdon's claims that the building was named after Pantheism, the true origin of its name comes from the fact that the temple was erected in praise of and for the whole "pantheon" of Roman gods.

The original Pantheon was built in 27 BC by the soldier and politician Marcus Agrippa to a quite different design, but this building burned down and was replaced by another temple under the Emperor Domitian. In AD 110 it burned down again due to a lightning strike, and this time it was left in the capable hands of the Emperor Hadrian to oversee the design and construction of a new, more decorative and sophisticated Pantheon. The result, completed in AD 125, is a monument that glorifies the technological and engineering expertise of the Roman architects and builders.

Entry to the Pantheon is gained through a columned portico, with each column 39 feet (11.9m) tall, 5 feet (1.5m) in diameter, and weighing 60 tonnes. The 16 granite columns were quarried in Egypt's eastern mountains and transported from there all the way to Rome. On the front of the portico, Hadrian had inscribed the words: M AGRIPPA L F COS TERTIUM FECIT ("Built by Marcus Agrippa, the son of Lucius, third consul"). A connecting vestibule leads to the enormous bronze doors that take the visitor directly into the circular rotunda topped by an impressive dome that features a circular opening, called the "oculus," measuring 29 feet (8.8m) in diameter and through which natural light enters the building. According to legend, when the temple was reconsecrated as a church, demons ascended through the oculus during the ceremony.

The rotunda's interior creates a perfect sphere, with its diameter of 142 feet (43.3m) equal to its height; this gives it a womblike quality entirely in keeping with the reverence that would once have been paid there to Gaea, the mother goddess. The building's walls are 20 feet (6.1m) thick and support the dome, which was built using tapering stepped rings of concrete that are thickest and heaviest at the base, and thinnest and lightest at the oculus. To help ease the weight on the upper courses of the dome, empty clay pots were embedded into its superstructure. The oculus also helps to lighten the load on the dome and is finished off with bronze edging.

Hidden arches embedded within the interior walls of the Pantheon also take the weight of the dome. These interior walls are on two levels. The upper level is decorated with false windows and frames, while the lower level consist of niches, which were originally filled with statues of the gods that were subsequently removed by the Church. These recesses now hold chapels and tombs—including the tomb of Raphael, which Langdon and Vittoria are so desperate to find, and which is located between the second and third chapel on the left on entry to the Pantheon.

See also: Bede, St; Gaea; Oculus; Raphael.

Papal Conclave

On taking the helicopter to Vatican City, Robert Langdon and Vittoria Vetra note the number of press vans positioned towards the rear of St Peter's Square. The pilot points out that all the attention is due to the imminent election of a new pope by the conclave. The fact that a great many cardinals are gathered at the Vatican for the conclave makes the threat from the hidden antimatter canister even more deadly. In bringing the cardinals together, the event has also provided the victims for the series of murders that will occur across the city of Rome. The succession from one pope to another will always be a hugely significant event for Catholics; in *Angels & Demons*, the enemies of the Church are trying to ensure that it has a wider global effect.

The first popes appointed their own successor, but this system subsequently changed and popes came to be elected by the clergy and the people of Rome. From the eleventh century, however, all popes have been elected by the cardinals. There was considerable disruption to Church business if the cardinals could not agree on a successor, and if elections were drawn out over an extended period. In the thirteenth century the papacy was vacant for one and a half years until Innocent IV was finally elected in 1243, and it was three and a half years until Gregory X was elected in 1271. In the 1243 election in Rome, the cardinals were eventually locked in a room until they chose a pope, and in 1271, in Viterbo, the cardinals were not only confined to a room, but the roof of the building was removed in an attempt to encourage a quicker conclusion by exposing them to the elements; they were also only also given bread and water until they eventually made their decision. The term "conclave" comes from this practice of locking away the cardinals: it's from the Latin *cum clavis*, meaning "with a key."

On the death of a pope, the Cardinal Camerlengo (chamberlain) takes control of the papal household. He also confirms the Pope's death by ceremonially striking the pontiff's forehead three times with a silver hammer, and calling out his birth name. The Pope's private apartments are locked and sealed by the camerlengo, and the papal Fisherman's ring and the seal on the ring are broken. No autopsy is performed on a dead pope. It is the camerlengo's duty to inform the Vicar of Rome of a pope's death, and he in turn notifies the people. Cardinals from around the world are then informed and must be within the Vatican before the start of conclave, fifteen days after the Pope's death. The funeral rites last nine days and are organized by the camerlengo and the three cardinals who head the cardinal orders (cardinal bishops, cardinal priests, and cardinal deacons). Together, these four cardinals also arrange the conclave.

Conclave includes all cardinals below the age of eighty years at the time of the Pope's death. Even cardinals who have been excommunicated have the right to attend. The number of cardinal electors was set at 70 in 1586, but this was increased to 120 in 1970 by Pope Paul VI. However, under the present Pope there are now 135 cardinals (not 165 as mentioned in *Angels & Demons*), so it is uncertain whether all cardinals will be allowed to attend, or whether the rules will be changed to accommodate the increased numbers. Once in conclave, no one can leave except in extreme circumstances, such as if a cardinal is taken ill. To ensure the cardinals' unbiased vote, all means of outside contact are removed from the rooms.

Where once conclave was limited to one room, it now covers up to three floors of the Vatican Palace; the area is divided into apartments, each with three or four small rooms that contain a crucifix, bed, table, and chairs. This is in order to accommodate certain officials who are also permitted to attend—each cardinal is allowed a secretary and a servant within conclave, and a nurse if necessary. All are sworn to secrecy and noninterference in the election. Also included in conclave are kitchen staff, the secretary of the college of cardinals, the master of papal liturgical celebrations, the Cardinal Camerlengo and two masters of ceremonies. In all there are approximately 250 people allowed within the enclosure. However, access to the Sistine Chapel, where the actual cardinal electors vote, is strictly regulated.

On the morning of conclave, the cardinal electors and the various attendants celebrate Mass in St Peter's Basilica. In the afternoon they congregate at the Pauline Chapel in the Apostolic Palace and from there they go to the Sistine Chapel, where they swear an oath of secrecy and noninterference. At this point, all those not connected with the election must leave the Sistine Chapel, which is closed to unauthorized personnel by the camerlengo. When the attendants have left, a prayer is said by a priest to remind the cardinals of their duty and he then leaves with the master of papal liturgical celebrations. The cardinal electors are now left alone to pray and vote in silence. At this time the first ballot is allowed, which must have a two-thirds majority for a pope to be elected. If this is not achieved the cardinals are allowed to go back to their rooms, and they return to the Sistine Chapel the following day.

During the balloting process the name of a cardinal is written on a card, which is folded in half. Each cardinal approaches the altar one at a time in order of precedence, depending on who has served as a cardinal the longest. They then kneel before the altar, holding up their folded vote, and say a short prayer. Upon standing the cardinal states: "I call as my witness Christ the Lord, who will be my judge, that my vote is given to the one who before God I think should be elected." The vote is then placed on a plate that sits on the altar, which is used to slide the vote into a chalice. This is to ensure that two votes are not cast at the same time.

The unfolded ballots are then counted by a scrutineer— one chosen from among the cardinals—who checks that the number of ballots matches the number of cardinals. The votes are then counted by two more scrutineers, who each write the names on separate sheets of paper. The sheets are handed to a fourth scrutineer who then reads the name out aloud and slides the ballot onto a threaded needle. Once the voting is completed, the ends of the thread are tied, and the votes for each candidate are counted. Three revisers then check the ballots and notes, eventually burning them, helped by the secretary of the conclave and the master of ceremonies. The smoke that is produced from the burning of the ballots then emerges from the chimney and is clearly visible to the expectant public waiting outside in St Peter's Square. Chemicals are used to make the smoke black— indicating an unsuccessful ballot—or white—to show the people that a pope has been elected. The only record of the voting is prepared by the camerlengo at the end of the election. The document is given to the new pontiff and placed in a sealed envelope in the archives. This may only be opened if permitted by the Pope.

Some of the early conclaves sat for over a month, but modern ones have been adapted so that they are generally settled within two weeks—and often less than that. Revisions to voting procedure mean that if a pope is not elected on the first day, the following day two ballots are held in the morning and two in the afternoon. If after the third day there is still no new pope the cardinals are allowed to take a day's break for prayer and discussions. It continues in this fashion for another twelve days, after which the camerlengo asks the electors whether they will accept an absolute majority vote or choose between two front-runners.

When a pope is eventually elected, the camerlengo asks if the chosen candidate accepts the election. Not all do accept this position—in 1978, for example, when the cardinal of Milan began to receive votes, he let it be known that he would decline the papacy if elected.

See also: Camerlengo; St Peter's Basilica; Sistine Chapel; Vatican, The.

PETER,ST

Peter, St

In *Angels & Demons*, the heart of the Catholic Church—the
Vatican in Rome—is under threat from an explosive device
hidden somewhere in the building. St Peter's Basilica within
the Vatican is built on the supposed site of the tomb of St
Peter, and the frantic search to locate the lethal canister of
antimatter leads the characters deep underground, to the
sarcophagus attributed to the apostle.

The fisherman Simon, along with his brother, Andrew,
became a disciple of Jesus, who named Simon "Rock"
(which corresponds to Peter—Petros in Greek). Peter
receives special mention in the Bible, one of the most
significant passages in this regard coming in St John's
Gospel 21:15: "Jesus said to Simon Peter, 'Simon, son of
Jonas, do you love me more than these [the other disciples]?'
He said to him, 'Yes, Lord, you know that I love you.' He
said to him, 'Feed my lambs.'"

This emotional, perhaps rather simple, man clearly had
tremendous faith, and after Christ's death played a leading
part in bringing the Christian message to the Roman world,
feeding the spiritual need felt by some of his
contemporaries for whom the older religions were no
longer satisfactory.

Jesus had stated that he would build his church on the
strong rock—i.e. Peter—and that the fisherman would be
given the keys of the Kingdom of Heaven. These are the
metaphorical keys of St Peter, still a papal symbol nearly
two millennia later. St Peter is thought to have become
Bishop of Antioch after decreeing that non-Jews could be
admitted to full Church membership without having to
obey all Mosaic Laws and Jewish customs.

It is commonly believed that Peter went to Rome and
was martyred, probably after the great fire of Rome, under
Nero. His body is supposed to have been preserved and a
shrine erected over it some twenty years later, which became
the site of St Peter's Basilica in the Vatican. (Peter is

regarded as the first of the popes.) Pope Paul VI declared that bones discovered under the altar of St Peter's Basilica during excavations in the 1940s were those of the saint, and they were reinterred on June 27, 1968.

The Gospel of St Peter is one of the books that comprise the Apocrypha.

See also: Apocrypha; Matthew 16:18; St Peter's Basilica; Vatican, The.

Pius IX, Pope

As head of the Catholic Church from 1846 to 1878, Pope Pius IX (1792-1878) has had the longest pontificate in history, and his leadership saw significant developments both in the political role of the Papal States (territories governed by the Church, mainly in central Italy), and in Church doctrine. As Robert Langdon and Vittoria Vetra hurry through the corridors of the Vatican, Dan Brown tells us that in 1857, Pius IX was responsible for castrating statues in the Vatican to preserve decency, an accusation that has proved difficult to verify. Indeed, when elected to the papacy, Pius IX was considered to be a liberal choice and one of his first actions was to declare an amnesty for political prisoners and exiles.

The political climate in Italy at that time was very volatile, and in 1848 the circumstances in Rome were so dangerous that after being forced into appointing lay ministers, Pius fled to Gaeta in the Kingdom of Naples. It was only with the help of the French that papal rule was re-established in Rome, and in 1850 Pius IX returned there.

The momentum for Italian unification was growing, and in 1870, after Italian troops occupied the city, Rome was incorporated into the Kingdom of Italy. Pius IX did not accept or recognize the new sovereignty, and it was not until the Lateran Treaty of 1929 that the papacy reached an accord with the state of Italy under the Fascist government of Benito Mussolini.

In doctrinal matters Pius IX's influence was significant. In 1854, the Immaculate Conception of the Blessed Virgin was declared as Church dogma, and in 1870, after some initial opposition, the dogma of papal infallibility was adopted at the First Vatican Council. Pius's initial liberalism turned to conservatism after the events of 1848, and in 1864 the Church published the encyclical *Quanta Cura*, condemning what Pius saw as the errors of the age. These included ideas such as communism, socialism, religious liberalism, and Freemasonry. There are unconfirmed reports that prior to his elevation to the papacy, the former Giovanni Maria Mastai-Ferretti had himself been a Freemason, but that he was expelled from the brotherhood after Italian unification.

See also: Freemasonry; Rome; Vatican, The.

Pranayama

Vittoria Vetra occasionally employs this yogic breathing technique to enable her to relax as the dramatic events unfold in *Angels & Demons*, for example when Olivetti locks her and Robert Langdon in his Vatican office. Langdon first learns about this relaxation method when he and Vittoria are preparing to enter the Pantheon in Rome, where they may risk a confrontation with the sinister figure who has kidnapped four cardinals.

Pranayama is a Sanskrit word meaning "breath control." In yoga it is the fourth of eight stages that lead a practitioner to the state of perfect concentration.

There are different types of pranayama, some of the most common being:

- Ujjayi—in which the mind can be focused by lengthening inhalation and exhalation;
- Dirgha—a three-part breath to fill the lower lungs, thoracic region, and clavicle area in turn, resulting in expulsion of carbon monoxide and oxygenation of the blood;
- Nadi Shodhana—a technique of breathing through each nostril alternately to soothe anxiety and stress.

Pranayama can be used alone, in preparation for meditation, or during asana (the practice of postures).

Pyramids

Having initially misinterpreted the first clue concerning Santi's tomb, Robert Langdon and Vittoria Vetra race off to the Church of Santa Maria del Popolo in search of the Chigi Chapel and the "demon's hole." Inside the Chigi Chapel—a Christian chapel designed by Raphael—Langdon is amazed to see two 10-foot (3m) marble pyramids. These pyramids mark the graves of two members of the Chigi family and were probably designed in this style because of the fashionable influence that ancient Egypt had on Roman architecture in the early sixteenth century.

Of all the ancient monuments of the world the pyramid is probably the most recognizable. The term "pyramid" is derived from a Greek word (*pyramis*), and is named for its similarity in shape to a Greek wheat cake. However, the Egyptian term for these colossal stone funerary monuments is *mer*, which has been translated as "Place of Ascension/Transformation." To the ancient Egyptians the pyramid symbolized the mound of Creation, the first piece of land to emerge out of the primeval waters. It also represented the first rays of the sun as they descended towards the earth to give life to all.

The most famous pyramids are to be found at Giza in Egypt, close to modern-day Cairo, though it is not certain that these were ever used for burial. The pyramids of Giza date to around 2500 BC, with the pharaoh Khufu's Great Pyramid the largest surviving example. It contains three burial chambers, one of which was subterranean and unfinished. Of the other two, the top chamber, known today as the King's Chamber, has airshafts leading to the exterior of the pyramid and is aligned with certain stars important to the ascension of the deceased pharaoh's soul. The middle chamber, known as the Queen's Chamber, also has shafts, and one of these appears to contain a metal door, albeit very small. As yet it is uncertain what lies beyond this barrier.

The other two large pyramids on the Giza Plateau are attributed to Khafra and Menkaura, the two successors of Khufu. There are also a number of subsidiary pyramids attributed to the queens of the pharaohs that form part of the complex, along with funerary and valley temples and causeways.

The first known pyramid is the Step Pyramid, thought to date to 2600 BC. This was built at Saqqara, south of Cairo, by the Third-Dynasty pharaoh Djoser and, as its name suggests, it was a flat-topped, stepped pyramid. Over time the step pyramid developed into the shape we now know, although not without some problems and experimentation.

Sneferu's Bent Pyramid at Dahshur (built 2613–2589 BC) changes angle partway up, no doubt due to the Egyptian builders' realization of the technical problems they would encounter if the original angle was maintained.

By the Fifth Dynasty (2494–2345 BC) the pyramids at Abusir, south of Giza, had become smaller in size and architecturally inferior, with smaller stone blocks replacing the monumental blocks of the earlier period. At this time, however, texts began to appear on the interior walls of pyramids for the first time. The innovator of these pyramid texts was the pharaoh Unas (2375–2345 BC), whose pyramid was inscribed with utterances or words to help protect him on his journey to the sky. These sacred words took the form of ritual spells, glorification spells, protection spells, hymns, litanies, and charms.

By the Eleventh Dynasty (2055–1985 BC), pyramids were being constructed from mud-brick infilled with rubble, and with their exterior cased in limestone. On completion they would have looked similar to their older counterparts, but once the outer casing was removed—as happened in later periods, when they were robbed of their easily available pre-cut limestone—the pyramids were soon reduced to rubble. Pyramid-building ceased after the Thirteenth Dynasty (1795–1650 BC approximately), by which time 35 pyramids had been constructed by the ancient Egyptians.

The love of pyramids has continued to the present day, throughout the world. Examples of modern pyramids include the large glass entrance pyramid to the Louvre, Paris, and the much smaller Pyramide Inversée near by, which acts as a skylight for an underground complex of shops and other facilities. The Louvre is an important location in Dan Brown's bestselling novel *The Da Vinci Code*, and the Pyramide Inversée provides the background for the climax to Robert Langdon's search for the Holy Grail.

See also: Chigi Chapel; Egyptian Religion; Santa Maria del Popolo.

Raphael

Also known as Raffaello Santi (or Sanzi)—though more commonly as simply Raphael—this famed Renaissance artist left a remarkable legacy to show for his short life. His tomb in the Pantheon, Rome, provides the first location on a breakneck tour of churches for Robert Langdon on his quest to rescue the hostage cardinals in *Angels & Demons*.

Born in Urbino in Italy in 1483, Raphael was the son of the painter Giovanni Santi, who introduced his son to the artistic and cultural influences of the humanist court of Federico da Montefeltro. Although a soldier by calling, Federico devoted his wealth to transforming Urbino into a town where artists, scholars, and musicians could thrive under his patronage. After the death of his father, Raphael traveled to Perugia, where he quickly established a reputation for himself. In a document from 1500 recording the commission of an altarpiece, he is referred to as a "master," meaning that he must have successfully established the quality of his work by that date. Raphael gained experience with the great Pietro Perugino, and his first major painting, *The Marriage of the Virgin*, was influenced by Perugino's style.

Further works—such as *The Three Graces* and *Vision of a Knight*—confirmed Raphael's ability to convey freshness and personality in his painting, but soon he was ready to move on from Perugia. By 1504, the presence in Florence of Leonardo da Vinci and Michelangelo had inspired Raphael to travel there, and he studied with both of these exceptional talents. He produced a series of paintings of Madonnas influenced by Leonardo's picture of *Madonna with Child and St Anne*, and using similar lighting techniques to Leonardo. Raphael also made use of Leonardo's *sfumato* (smoked) method of painting, in which soft shading is used to delineate features, producing a more sensitive interpretation. His work *The Deposition of Christ* revealed that Raphael had also learned from Michelangelo's

RAPHAEL

representation of anatomy. Despite the obvious influence of
the other masters, however, Raphael showed qualities of
calmness and serenity in his paintings that make them stand
out. His talents rapidly became more widely known, and in
1508 Pope Julius II invited him to Rome, at the suggestion
of the architect Donato Bramante.

The Stanza della Segnatura, in the Vatican papal
apartments, was decorated with frescoes by Raphael, the
most famous of which is *The School of Athens*: Plato and
Aristotle, surrounded by other philosophers in a variety of
gestures and poses, stand in an architectural background
similar to Bramante's plans for the new basilica of St Peter's
at the Vatican. A series of ten tapestries was commissioned
for the Sistine Chapel by the succeeding pope, Leo X, who
also appointed Raphael to work with Bramante on the
basilica. After Bramante's death, Raphael assumed control
of the project to rebuild St Peter's Basilica, making
additions to the plans. The Pope's interest in classical
sculpture led to him making Raphael responsible for the
preservation of all marble statues bearing Latin
inscriptions, and in 1517 he became Commissioner of
Antiquities for Rome.

Raphael also undertook work for other clients, including
the Chigi family, for whom he designed a chapel in the
Church of Santa Maria del Popolo, the location of the first
of the cardinals' murders in *Angels & Demons*. At the time
of his death Raphael was working on *The Transfiguration*, an
altarpiece that was finished by his pupil Giulio Romano.

In 1520, at the age of just 37 (not 38, as Robert Langdon
asserts), Raphael died in Rome and his funeral mass was
held at the Vatican, with *The Transfiguration* placed at the
head of the coffin. There may be an irony in this devout
funeral, as the sixteenth-century biographer Giorgio Vasari
is quoted as saying that Raphael was an atheist, an idea to
which Langdon makes reference in *Angels & Demons*.

Originally buried under the statue of the Madonna del

Sasso that he had commissioned, Raphael's body was exhumed in 1833 and reburied in its current location in the Pantheon; a bust of the artist by Giuseppe Fabris was erected in a niche above the tomb. Raphael's body rests next to that of his fiancée, Maria de Bibiena, who had died before they could marry. His epitaph reads: "Here lies Raphael, by whom the mother of all things [nature] feared to be overcome whilst he was living, and whilst he was dying, herself to die."

See also: Chigi Chapel; Michelangelo; Pantheon, The; St Peter's Basilica; Vatican, The.

Rome

Most of the action in *Angels & Demons* takes place in Rome, seat of the Vatican, and the city provides the locations for the frantic hunt for clues to save the spiritual center of the Catholic Church.

The city is named for the legendary ruler Romulus, who is credited with its foundation in 753 BC. He became Rome's first king and chose the Palatine Hill on which to build his settlement, where it is said he killed his twin, Remus, in a quarrel. This hill eventually became the seat of imperial government.

The last King of Rome, Tarquin the Proud, was expelled in 509 BC, and a republic was established. Two consuls ruled each year, advised by the aristocratic Senate and assisted by annually elected magistrates. These nobles, or patricians as they were called, were forced during the later centuries to cede some of their power to the plebeians (non-aristocrats) who, while often rich and influential, were not of the ancient stock who had traditionally occupied the offices of government. Elected tribunes, intended to protect the common citizens' interests, gradually broke down the dominance of the Senate and the people began to enjoy better economic conditions.

However, the early Romans were by no means powerful or secure. In 390 BC, invading Gauls sacked the city, although they allegedly failed to take the Capitoline Hill. This disaster spurred the fledgling nation to undertake pre-emptive wars of conquest and domination against its neighbors, using a conscripted citizen army. Colonies were founded and tributes extracted that enriched the city when alliances were demanded of defeated peoples.

So successful were these policies that by the end of 167 BC virtually the whole Mediterranean area was subject to Roman authority, following victories against the Carthaginians and the Hellenistic kingdoms of Asia and Greece. After the Third Punic War (149–146 BC) the city of Carthage was obliterated and North Africa became a province of Rome, as did Macedonia.

Military conquests provided, among other assets, plentiful slaves. Landowners were able to cultivate land cheaply with slave labor, but peasant farmers, already subject to military service, suffered: the unfair competition led to many of them losing their livelihood and falling into extreme poverty, with attendant adverse consequences for the citizen army. The rich grew immensely wealthy; the poor lost the little they had. Attempts by the Gracchus brothers—who were tribunes—and their supporters to amend the situation and restore some measure of justice failed, and both the brothers had been murdered by 121 BC.

Financially draining wars against the Germans, the Africans of Numidia, and against their Italian neighbors provided a shock to the equanimity of prosperous Romans.

In order to deal with the threat to the state and its less-than-efficient government, it became increasingly necessary to create a professional army led by ambitious men.

By 49 BC, two such men—Julius Caesar and Pompey the Great—had become the leaders of opposing factions within Rome, and their battle for control plunged the state into civil war. The former was fresh from his conquest of Gaul and he emerged triumphant over Pompey, with new dictatorial powers. Fearing Caesar's position had now become too dangerously powerful, conspirators, including Brutus and Cassius, murdered him. Further civil wars broke out between those wishing to avenge Caesar and those anxious to preserve the republic or enhance their own positions.

Caesar's nephew and heir, the wily and unscrupulous Augustus—at that time known as Octavian—won the struggle for power, largely thanks both to his Caesarian connections and to the loyal and extremely able lieutenant Marcus Vipsanius Agrippa. In 31 BC Augustus's great rival, Mark Antony, was defeated, despite his support from Queen Cleopatra of Egypt, and Augustus became the first Emperor of Rome—or more properly the Princeps. He cunningly took over all the important powers of the state, voted to him by a servile and subservient Senate whom he flattered and honored with honeyed words. Augustus now had ultimate authority over all Roman territories and armed forces, the wealth of the land of Egypt—which became his own kingdom quite separate from the empire—and most importantly took the power of a tribune (or ruler) for life, giving him a veto over all laws. His tact did, however, lead him to defer adopting the title Pontifex Maximus (literally, "great bridge builder" or "supreme priest") until 13 BC, on the death of Lepidus, who had held the post for the previous 31 years. Despite the fact that Romans of Augustus's generation and of generations for many centuries to come continued to refer to the state as a republic it had, in fact, become a monarchy.

Augustus liked to create the illusion that his power came entirely by consent of the Senate and the people, but in reality both he and his successors held the supreme office only by sufferance of the military. A successful mutiny by a strategically placed army could topple an emperor and replace him with a leader more to the soldiers' taste— usually one who had promised them financial inducements.

After such an aggressive policy of expansion, the benefits of consolidating the existing borders of the empire now became apparent. Romans enjoyed the peace, called the Pax Romana, and were extraordinarily skillful at allowing those whose territory was annexed to carry on using their own language, customs, and lifestyle with little hindrance from the national government, providing that taxes were paid and loyal sentiments to the empire— personified by the Emperor himself—were expressed. Since the Romans had no "jealous gods," religious tolerance was almost universal, provided that the authorities' sense of decency was not offended. Generally the Jews had special arrangements made for them to be exempted from those aspects of public life that offended their religion and laws. However, because of their strongly held beliefs they occasionally found themselves in conflict—at times very bloody conflict—with their masters, and also the Christians with whom they had much in common but from whom they became increasingly estranged.

In the third century AD barbarian invasions led to the abandonment of territory north of the rivers Danube and Rhine. The city of Rome gradually started to lose its importance and the eastern half of the empire began to dominate. By then the Emperors themselves were less likely to be Italian than Syrians, Africans, or Slavs. Coming from the further reaches of the empire many never set eyes on the city of Rome at all. Central government emanated from wherever the Emperor happened to be, while local communities looked after their own routine affairs with much independence within the overall framework of taxation, trade, and defense.

During the fourth century, the Emperor Constantine realized the potential value of a unifying state religion supervised by himself and flirted with the idea that the supreme god should be Sol, the unconquered solar power. He issued coins depicting this deity and declared Sol to be patron of his dynasty. It became obvious to him, however, that the Christian Church had a useful hierarchy and a structure that was superior to anything the fragmented pagan faiths had to offer. He decided to promote Christianity for his own purposes, therefore, favoring Christian officials and the spread of their religion. His mother was already a devotee although he himself was not baptized until he knew he was dying so that, with his sins washed away, he could be assured of a place in Heaven. Among these sins were the murders of a wife and a son.

The Christian Church had many factions that developed their own beliefs and practices as the disciples, and subsequent followers of Christ, preached His message. For example, in Alexandria, Egypt, traditions were established that developed into the Coptic Church, still active in Egypt and elsewhere today. The Catholic Church preserved a tradition of a direct line of Bishops of Rome, starting with the apostle St Peter, one of Jesus's disciples. The supremacy of the Bishop of Rome over all other bishops in the Catholic Church was established, and led to the adoption of the title previously used in the pagan religion, Pontifex Maximus. The name by which we now recognize the Bishop of Rome, i.e. Pope (from the late [ecclesiastical] Latin *papa*, meaning "bishop"; from the Greek *papas*, meaning "bishop" or "patriarch"; originally from the Greek *pappas*, meaning "father") is believed to have first been used by Pope Siricius in AD 384. After Christianity became adopted in the Roman Empire, the papacy was given civic authority within the state in addition to its religious authority. The so-called Papal States were created when additional land was added to Rome to reinforce the status of the Pope as a secular and religious leader.

In the early fourth century Constantine the Great established a new capital city at Byzantium, now known as Istanbul, modestly naming it Constantinople (Constantine's city). It was to be the new Rome. In 395 the empire was again split into eastern and western halves under the brothers Honorius and Arcadius. The ineffective Honorius made Ravenna the capital of the western empire, as Rome was too accessible to potential invaders. The venerable city of Rome was sacked by the Visigoths of Alaric in the year 410 and again by the Vandals under Gaiseric in 455, and throughout the fifth and sixth centuries Rome changed hands several times.

It was Pope Gregory I (ruled 590–604) who used the temporal power of the papacy to begin to restore the city's fortunes. He encouraged pilgrims to visit the relics contained in Rome, and the penitents brought their wealth with them. The revival was continued with the coronation of the Frank (i.e. French) King Charlemagne as Holy Roman Emperor a couple of centuries later, meaning that a powerful European leader with a vast empire was answerable to the Pope, and therefore owed the city some protection.

There were, of course, setbacks, and when a Frenchman was elected as Pope Clement V, under the patronage of the French crown, he relocated the papacy to Avignon in France in 1305. The loss of income from visitors damaged the city that had been living in the shadow of the Church organization, and the population of Rome dramatically declined.

Against the wishes of the nobility, the citizens of Rome adopted Cola di Rienzo as a leader, and he proclaimed a new republic in 1347 with high expectations and popular support. Once in power, however, Rienzo, who had adopted the ancient title of "tribune," became dictatorial, and his dreams of an Italian empire with Rome as its capital earned him many enemies. He was deposed and eventually murdered, and in 1377 Gregory XI returned the papal seat to Rome and ushered in a new papacy that flourished during the Renaissance.

The city of Rome benefited from the patronage of the families that pledged allegiance to the papal throne and spent large sums of money enriching itself. Churches were built or restored as each pope tried to outshine his predecessor, and during the Renaissance many of the finest artists, architects, and sculptors—including Raphael, Michelangelo, and Donato Bramante—were employed to decorate the public and private spaces of Rome. Playing a political game of allying themselves with whichever European power they thought most advantageous, the Renaissance popes were in many cases cynical, and some, such as Leo X (ruled 1513–22)—who sold indulgences and Church positions—were downright corrupt. In 1527 Clement VII was forced to take refuge in Castel Sant'Angelo as the armies of the Holy Roman Emperor Charles V sacked and occupied Rome for almost a year, in an echo of its earlier history.

Another period of restoration and ornamentation followed. The seventeenth century saw artists such as Gian Lorenzo Bernini given commissions by successive popes to build churches, palaces, and fountains, while at the heart of the city, the Basilica of St Peter's at the Vatican was redesigned. Rome declined in political importance and a brief invasion by Napoleon in 1796 resulted in papal rule being suspended until 1815, after Napoleon's own final defeat. Italian nationalist movements were suppressed, and it was not until 1870 that the revolutionary conqueror Giuseppe Garibaldi was able to declare Rome the capital of the new Kingdom of Italy under Victor Emmanuel II.

Rome was now the capital city of a new state, and this

heralded another phase of public building as new streets were constructed to make circulation easier, and national ministry buildings were erected. Benito Mussolini signed an agreement called the Lateran Treaty with Pope Pius XI in 1929, which recognized the Vatican as a sovereign territory. The Second World War left the city relatively undamaged—since it was declared an "open city," and therefore spared a pitched battle—as the Allies advanced toward it.

After the abdication of the King after the war, Rome remained the capital city of the Italian Republic, and as the home of the Vatican State it therefore has the distinction of being two capital cities in one. No longer the center of a huge empire, the city of Rome has slowly metamorphosed into something even more all-embracing. Since, with short exceptions, it has continuously housed the popes, the Roman Catholic Church has been guided from the "Eternal City" for around 2,000 years. Millions of believers around the world look towards it, and it is this aspect of Rome's importance on which Dan Brown has chosen to focus in *Angels & Demons*.

See also: Castel Sant'Angelo; St Peter's Basilica; Vatican, The.

St Peter's Basilica

Much of *Angels & Demons* is set within St Peter's Basilica or its immediate environs. In the course of the book, Robert Langdon can be found within its corridors and private apartments, the holy church, and the Vatican Library, as well as the gardens and, of course, St Peter's Square, where—at the base of Caligula's Egyptian obelisk—the murder of the second cardinal takes place.

To enter St Peter's Basilica it is first necessary to cross St Peter's Square, built between 1656 and 1667. The square was designed by Gian Lorenzo Bernini and is a huge ellipse with its perimeter edged by two enormous colonnades supported by four parallel rows of 284 Doric columns, each 60 feet (18.3m) tall. Above these are 140 statues of saints, who look down on to the square. Within the ellipse is an obelisk, flanked by two fountains—one designed by Carlo Maderno in 1613 and the other by Bernini in 1675. St Peter's Square is large enough to accommodate 300,000 people comfortably, although it often holds more.

The original basilica of St Peter's was built by Constantine the Great, the first Christian Emperor of Rome. It was completed in AD 349 on the site of the Vatican Hill, where St Peter was supposed to have been buried in AD 64. The present basilica was built in the sixteenth and seventeenth centuries to replace and improve upon the former building. The chief architect was Donato Bramante, but later Michelangelo took over the project, becoming chief architect in 1546 and designing the dome as well as altering some of the original designs. It was finally completed in 1626, 120 years after the first stone was laid by Pope Julius II.

St Peter's Basilica is the world's second largest church, its nave being 715 feet (218m) long, its dome 138 feet (42m) in diameter and 443 feet (135m) high. It contains 45 altars, and houses many chapels, tombs, and works of art by such artists as Michelangelo, Bernini, and Antonio Canova. Above the façade of the basilica are statues of Jesus, John the Baptist, and eleven of the apostles. The statue of St Peter is inside.

A portico designed by Maderno leads to the three entrance doors, the central set having been taken from the original basilica. Immediately inside the basilica on the right is Michelangelo's *Pietà*, a statue that depicts Mary the Mother of Jesus holding her son after he has been taken down from the Cross. This now sits behind a protective glass screen, after an attack on it in the 1980s. Probably the most sought-out statue in the basilica is *St Peter Enthroned*, alleged to be the work of the thirteenth-century sculptor Arnolfo di Cambio. The statue's right foot has been worn down over the centuries by the kisses of pilgrims and visitors.

The most impressive sight in the basilica, however, has to be the main altarpiece of *St Peter in Glory*, situated beneath Michelangelo's dome and above the purported tomb of St Peter. On entering the basilica it is impossible to miss the enormous baldachin (an ornate canopy) that stands over the main altar. Designed by Bernini, the 85-feet-high (26m) bronze baldachin is supported by four massive spiraling pillars that were cast in 1633 out of metal taken from the roof of the Pantheon. Excavations beneath the baldachin have revealed Roman tombs, indicating that the area was once a burial site. One badly damaged tomb corresponded to an early description of St Peter's shrine. Near to this were found the bones of a fit, elderly man, which Pope Paul VI declared to be the bones of St Peter. However, it is not possible to verify whether these are indeed the remains of the saint, as the bones have never been scrutinized scientifically, nor carbon dated.

Michelangelo's dome is slightly smaller than that of the Pantheon. Along the base of its interior are 6.5-foot-high (2m) letters in Latin quoting Matthew 16:18–19: "You are Peter and on this rock I will build my church. . . I will give you the keys of the kingdom of heaven." The dome's four supporting piers are each decorated with a different relief. The pier bearing a relief of St Helena contains a piece of the True Cross; that of St Longinus contains the Spear of Destiny—the spear that pierced Jesus's side; that which depicts St Andrew contains the saint's skull; and the pier bearing a relief of St Veronica contains the veil that she used to wipe Jesus's face, according to popular legend.

Also within the basilica is the Treasury, which contains artifacts from the earlier church as well as a variety of monuments, including a tabernacle by Donatello. Beneath Bernini's statue of St Longinus are steps that lead down to the catacombs where many of the Popes are buried.

See also: Bernini, Gian Lorenzo; Matthew 16:18; Pantheon, The; Peter, St.

Santa Maria della Vittoria

This church has its entrance on Via XX Settembre in Rome, and is one of the most ornate churches in a city where splendor is on display at every turn. This busy street houses huge buildings, such as the Finance Ministry, which contrasts with its description in *Angels & Demons* as a remote location to which an embarrassing piece of art was banished. Dan Brown places the church on the Piazza Barberini, which is about 300 yards (274m) away from its real-life location, and states that the obelisk that once stood in the Piazza was moved when the subway was being built. In fact, the obelisk was moved in 1822, to the Pincio Gardens, where it can still be admired.

Originally named for St Paul, the church was renamed to celebrate victory after the Battle of White Mountain in 1620, at Prague, in which the chaplain had carried a picture of the Nativity as a talisman. At this battle, a Catholic force defeated the Czechs, whose political and religious freedoms were subsequently suppressed for nearly three hundred years.

In *Angels & Demons*, Dan Brown stages a pyre in the church, with pews providing the fuel for a terrible bonfire that has tragic consequences. There was, in fact, a real fire in the church in 1833, during which the painting of the Nativity was destroyed, but a copy is now positioned above the altar, and the Baroque interior was subsequently restored.

Cardinal Scipione Borghese financed the building of the church in 1608; the construction was supervised by Carlo Maderno, who had designed the Church of Santa Susanna near by. Giovanni Soria added the façade in 1626, but the main attraction in Santa Maria della Vittoria is the Cornaro Chapel, located on the left-hand side of the nave. This was designed by Gian Lorenzo Bernini and features his statue of *The Ecstasy of St Teresa*, in an elaborate design that incorporates marble depictions of the Cornaro family watching from theater boxes.

St Teresa is represented as being visited by an angel who carries a spear that is described in her autobiography as bearing a "touch of fire on its point." Bernini has illuminated the statue with light reflected from a hidden window, in a technique adapted from stage design. The choir gallery is supported by angels, and was designed by Mattia de' Rossi, who worked with Bernini.

See also: Bernini, Gian Lorenzo; Ecstasy of St Teresa, The.

Santa Maria del Popolo

At one corner of the Piazza del Popolo is the Church of Santa Maria del Popolo. Traditionally regarded as the location where Nero's ashes were buried—as well as being the site of the tombs of Nero's family, the Domitia—the area was cleared by Pope Paschal II, who erected a chapel on the site in 1099 to sanctify the ground. Robert Langdon and Vittoria Vetra come here to solve a clue and discover the body of a dead cardinal; the church becomes the first in a series of murder sites related to the four elements—in the case of the Church of Santa Maria del Popolo, the element is earth.

Pope Paschal's chapel was augmented over the years. Pope Sixtus IV added a monastery, which Martin Luther stayed in during his visit to Rome in 1511. Luther was disgusted by the corruption that he observed in Rome, and his subsequent teachings resulted in the Protestant Reformation.

On the orders of Pope Alexander VII, Bernini altered the façade of the church in the seventeenth century in favor of a Baroque style. Inside the church itself, the work of some of Italy's greatest artists adorns the different chapels. In the Cerasi Chapel are two paintings by Caravaggio—*The Conversion of St Paul* and *The Crucifixion of St Peter*. The Chigi Chapel was designed by Raphael and contains sculptures by Bernini, including *Habakkuk and the Angel*. In the Costa Chapel, Giovanni Borgia—one of the sons of the Borgia Pope Alexander VI—is buried, with his mother, as a reminder of historical papal indiscretions. The Rovere Chapel is embellished with frescoes by Pinturicchio, who also provided scenes from the Virgin's life in another side chapel. The stained glass in the apse was created by Guillaume de Marcillat in 1509, and is the oldest stained glass in Rome.

See also: Bernini, Gian Lorenzo; Chigi Chapel; Habakkuk and the Angel; Raphael.

Seraph

The trail Robert Langdon and Vittoria Vetra follow around Rome is dominated by the presence of angels, each of which points the way to the next clue or location. The form of the angel that accompanies St Teresa in the famous Bernini sculpture *The Ecstasy of St Teresa* is accepted to be that of a seraph, particularly as it is the word she uses in her own writings.

This word is normally used as the singular of seraphim, and derives from a Hebrew phrase, meaning, "to burn." The seraph are common to Judaic, Christian, and Islamic tradition. Sometimes described as having two or three pairs of wings, they are often seen as guardians of the throne of God. In the Old Testament Book of Isaiah, the mythical seraphim are creatures with six wings. Isaiah's visions of the afterlife included a host of seraphim, standing on each side of the heavenly throne as guardians and said to be human in form.

Seraphim are occasionally known as "the burning ones," or "the shining ones" (in the Book of Numbers, "seraph" denotes a fiery serpent, possibly meaning a poisonous creature), and are considered to be one of the highest-ranking celestial beings in the Christian hierarchy of angels. They are not to be confused with cherubs or cherubim, who seem to have played a different angelic role.

Modern scholars have postulated that the word "seraphim" may derive from the Babylonian word *sharrapu*, which was associated with Nargul, the fire god; alternatively, it may possibly derive from the Egyptian word *seref*, which was used to describe griffinlike creatures that guarded the tombs at Beni Hasan.

See also: Ecstasy of St Teresa, The.

Shaitan

In Arabic, the Devil is known as Iblis, and is also called Ash-shaytan (or As-shaitan); in Judaic and Christian legend, this character is known as Satan. At the beginning of *Angels & Demons*, Robert Langdon tells Maximilian Kohler that the Vatican denounced the growing anti-Christian Illuminati brotherhood as "Shaitan", because of its supposed opposition to the Church; similarly, many conspiracy theorists argue that the Illuminati are devil-worshipers or Satanists. There appears to be some confusion in this association, which may be explained by the meaning of the word "Shaitan" having changed somewhat through history. "Shaitan"/"Satan" originally seems to have meant "adversary," or even "questioner" in the original Hebrew; its associations with evil came later.

Shaitan is also known from the Qu'ran, where he is a whisperer of evil suggestions and thoughts into men's ears and hearts, though he seems to have no real control over the world of mankind, being able only to tempt and cajole people into evil deeds. Islamic legend has it that the angels were ordered to lie prostrate for Adam when he was created by Allah. All the angels obeyed this order except Shaitan, who argued that since Allah had created Adam from clay and himself from the flames of fire, that he (Shaitan) was better than Adam. Upon hearing this, Allah condemned Shaitan to Hell, but after Shaitan pleaded with him, Allah postponed his judgment. Thus, Shaitan's avowed aim is to lead the sons of Adam astray, misleading all but the most devoted followers of Allah, and so fill Hell with the misguided men who followed him. Shaitan is known as the source of all evil in the world.

Shaitans are also a class of Jinn, or spirits, in Islamic myth and legend. The Arab writer al-Jahiz outlined the system of evil Jinn, labeling them as unbelieving spirits. Other tales from folklore describe the Shaitans as exceptionally ugly creatures of either sex who can attain human form, although their feet remain cloven-hoofed. They are described as existing in a place between light and dark, being spreaders of disease, and living on excrement.

The role of the Shaitans in Islamic tradition seems to have been borrowed from Judaic lore, with these creatures sometimes assuming the role of very knowledgeable Jinn who are not necessarily evil. This seems to echo Judaic myth, which ascribes the role of questioner to Satan.

See also: Illuminati; Langdon, Robert; Lucifer; Vatican, The.

Sistine Chapel

The Sistine Chapel is probably one of the Vatican's most illustrious sites, after St Peter's Basilica itself, made famous by Michelangelo's renowned ceiling and wall paintings that depict the Creation, themes from the Old Testament, and the Last Judgment. It has been estimated that on average a staggering 15,000 people visit the Sistine Chapel daily. A large rectangular structure built between 1473 and 1481 for Pope Sixtus IV, it was intended to be a private papal chapel, and today it still fulfills this role. However, it is better known as the place where the conclave of cardinals convenes in order to elect a new pope, as described in *Angels & Demons*.

The wall paintings on one side of the Sistine Chapel depict the life of Moses; those on the other, the life of Jesus. The wall paintings were completed by the famous Renaissance artists Pietro Perugino (*Moses' Journey into Egypt; Jesus Giving St Peter the Keys to Heaven; The Baptism of*

Christ), Sandro Botticelli (*The Trial of Moses; The Punishment of the Rebels; Cleansing the Leper*), Cosimo Rosselli (*The Crossing of the Red Sea; Moses and the Law; The Last Supper; The Sermon on the Mount*), Luca Signorelli (*The Testament and Death of Moses*), Matteo de Lecce (*The Fight over the Body of Moses*), Arrigo Palludano (*The Resurrection of Christ*), Domenico Ghirlandaio (*The Calling of St Peter and St Andrew*), and Michelangelo (*The Last Judgment*).

Michelangelo's ceiling frescoes were commissioned by Pope Julius II, and work started on them in 1508. The frescoes show 39 scenes from the Old Testament, including *The Creation of Light, The Temptation and Expulsion from the Garden of Eden*, and *The Story of the Flood. The Creation of Adam* is probably the most famous of all the Sistine Chapel's ceiling frescoes, depicting God's outstretched index finger sending the spark of life to Adam's finger.

About 20 years after the completion of his ceiling frescoes, Michelangelo painted *The Last Judgment* on the wall behind the altar. The task took him five years to complete, as he insisted on working without any help from his staff. *The Last Judgment* depicts the resurrection of the dead and their day of reckoning before Jesus, who furiously points at the damned, destined for the agonies that await them in Hell. Michelangelo also depicts the angels who blow their trumpets to awaken the condemned and haul them by ropes or by the nape of the neck to stand before Jesus. Even before the painting was finished there were many who voiced their dislike of it, arguing that it was offensive to display so many naked bodies in the Pope's private chapel. Michelangelo's disdain of such remarks found an outlet within his work: he depicted his most vocal detractor, the papal master of ceremonies Biagio da Cesena, as Hell's doorkeeper, complete with donkey's ears.

See also: Michelangelo; Papal Conclave; St Peter's Basilica; Vatican, The.

Sol Invictus

This Latin name for the sun god literally translates as the "unconquered sun," and sun worship provided a link between many religions of the ancient world. Rome originally had a cult of Sol Indiges, who was worshiped alongside the moon goddess Luna, with an annual sacrifice on August 9. As Robert Langdon explains when recalling a lecture he had given to his students at Harvard, however, it was the later worship of Sol Invictus that provided a link with Christianity. Langdon and Vittoria visit the Pantheon in Rome and notice that some of the tombs there are aligned on an east-west axis, recalling the sun worship characteristic of pre-Christian religions.

There were many sun gods in the ancient Near East, and it was the importation of a Syrian form of the god that led to the increasing popularity of the Sol Invictus in Rome. In AD 218, a priest of the temple of Baal of Emesa, in Syria, was made Emperor of Rome and took the name Elagabalus. This young man built a temple to Sol Invictus on the Palatine in Rome and tried to establish his cult as the main religion, bringing the black cult stone to Rome. Unfortunately for Elagabalus, his libido was the most pronounced feature of his reign, and after less than four years in power he was assassinated as his debauchery became unacceptable.

In AD 274, the Emperor Aurelian made a new attempt to elevate the status of the Sol Invictus, whom he credited with helping him achieve military victories. He erected a large temple in the Campus Agrippae in Rome and depicted the Sol on his coins, a practice that was continued by his successors. When Constantine the Great was looking to consolidate the faiths of his diverse empire into one religion it seemed at one point that he would choose Sol Invictus, and "Sol Invicto Comiti," meaning "committed to the invincible sun," was inscribed on his coins. Constantine eventually opted for Christianity instead, although he also incorporated elements of the popular cult of Mithras and Sol Invictus. Deis Solis, or Sunday, was henceforth considered to be a Mithraic day of rest, and December 25 was adopted as Christmas Day, having previously been held sacred for the birth of the sun.

In his book *Jesus: The Evidence*, Ian Wilson gives an example of how different traditions still coexisted alongside each other during the early days of Christianity: "A third-century mosaic from the mausoleum of the Julii, underneath present-day St Peter's in Rome, actually portrays Jesus as Sol Invictus, driving the horses of the sun god's chariot."

See also: Helios and Poseidon; Rome; St Peter's Basilica.

Swiss Guard

The Swiss Guard plays an integral role in *Angels & Demons* because of its function as the main security service for the Vatican. Robert Langdon calls them "the sworn sentinels of Vatican City" and is ambivalent about the Guards throughout the book, never quite sure if they are on the same side as him.

As the name suggests, the Swiss Guard is recruited from the cantons of Switzerland, and along with certain ceremonial duties its main task is to protect Vatican City and the Pope. It consists of 100 men who have to be Roman Catholic, under 30 years of age, and at least 5 foot 8 inches (1.7m) tall. To be acceptable, recruits must have completed their initial military training in the Swiss armed forces, and have obtained a certificate of good conduct. The length of service is usually two years but this can be extended in certain circumstances. The unique ceremonial uniform of the Swiss Guard is based upon a Renaissance design, and is believed by some to have been the work of Michelangelo, although the uniform was simplified in 1914. Wearing plumed metal helmets, blue, red, and yellow tunics, pantaloons, and gaiters, the Swiss Guard makes an impressive and distinctive sight.

The guardsmen's duties begin on May 6 (in commemoration of the Sack of Rome, which occurred on that date) when new recruits are sworn in, pledging an oath of absolute loyalty to the Pope. When a recruit is sworn in, he raises three fingers of his right hand to signify the Holy Trinity of Father, Son, and Holy Spirit, while his left hand holds the flag of the Swiss Guard Corps. From then on, the Guards serve as the Pope's personal bodyguard, whether in plain clothes— when the Pope is moving around in a crowd, for example—or in their colorful uniforms when on official guard duties at various points throughout Vatican City, including in front of the Pope's private apartment, at the great bronze door to the basilica, and at the Pope's General Audiences.

Switzerland has had a long history of providing mercenaries, and from the fifteenth century its soldiers of fortune were highly regarded for their courage, loyalty, and superior tactics. As such, they helped to shape Europe by taking part in the wars of France and Germany, as well as those of the Italian states. In 1497, Pope Sixtus IV made an alliance with the Swiss Confederation to recruit Swiss mercenaries in times of need, and with this in mind Sixtus IV built barracks to house them within what is today the confines of Vatican City. On January 22, 1506, at the invitation of Pope Julius II, a contingent of 150 Swiss mercenaries officially entered Rome, receiving a formal blessing from the Pope at a ceremony in St Peter's Square and thus becoming the Swiss Guard. In 1512 Pope Julius II bestowed on them the title "Defenders of the Church's

Freedom." This title was put to the test in a dramatic way during the Sack of Rome on May 6, 1527, when after becoming embroiled in a political conflict between Spain and France, Pope Clement VII was unable to defend the city from mercenaries fighting for Charles V of Spain. On that day German and Spanish troops broke through into St Peter's, and despite fighting desperately only 42 of the 189 Swiss Guards survived. Pillaging, plundering, and killing on a massive scale followed over the next eight days, resulting in 12,000 deaths and the destruction of many relics and works of art. Upon Pope Clement VII's surrender, and after being besieged in Castel Sant'Angelo, the papal garrison was replaced and although the remaining 42 Swiss Guards were allowed to rejoin the garrison, only 12 did so. Other terms of the surrender included the payment of a huge fine and the loss of territory, including the cities of Parma and Modena. It was only with the restoration of papal independence that the Swiss Guard regained their position as guardians of the Vatican.

In modern times, it was the Swiss Guard who protected Pope John Paul II during a failed assassination attempt in 1981 in St Peter's Square. In 1998 the commandant of the Swiss Guard was killed by a fellow guardsman, who then committed suicide. Officially explained as the result of a minor disagreement that escalated beyond control, there has been speculation that the commandant—Alois Estermann—was a member of Opus Dei. This shadowy, ultra-orthodox Catholic organization is featured in Dan Brown's novel *The Da Vinci Code*, and its background is explained further in my own *Cracking the Da Vinci Code*.

The 1874 constitution of Switzerland put an end to the practice of recruiting Swiss mercenaries, and Switzerland now has a famous reputation for neutrality in world affairs, although an exception is made for the Swiss Guard.

See also: Castel Sant'Angelo; Vatican, The.

Vatican, The

Maximilian Kohler sends Robert Langdon and Vittoria Vetra to Rome after he receives word from the Swiss Guard that the missing canister containing the deadly antimatter is somewhere within Vatican City. From there Langdon and Vittoria follow a trail of clues and symbols, which they hope will lead them to the missing cardinals and, ultimately, to the stolen antimatter.

The area now known as the Vatican was the place on the west bank of the River Tiber in Rome where St Peter was reputedly martyred, and is one of fourteen sections into which the Emperor Augustus divided the city. Two major highways, the Via Cornelia and the Via Triumphalis, run through this area and in ancient times these were lined with mausoleums and less imposing tombs. Excavations carried out under St Peter's Basilica in the 1940s revealed a tomb in which the remains of a burial were found. During a broadcast in December 1950, Pope Pius XII claimed that this was the tomb of St Peter, a belief that was later supported by Pope Paul VI. The authenticity of the bones, however, has never been properly established.

The Emperor Constantine the Great approved the creation of St Peter's Basilica on a massive terrace in the clay soil of the Vatican hill early in the fourth century. This structure was rebuilt in the sixteenth century and completed over the next hundred years with work by artists such as Bramante, Michaelangelo, and Bernini.

Mary the Mother of Christ holds a prominent place in the psyche of the Roman Catholic Church today and interestingly, altars believed to be for the worship of the pagan goddess Magna Mater—"the great mother"—have been identified on the site of St Peter's. This deity was imported, like Christianity, from the east into Rome, her sacred black stone being brought to the city as early as 204 BC.

The nearly triangular Vatican City—an independent state within the city of Rome—is today all that remains of the huge tracts of territory once ruled over by medieval popes, who reigned as worldly princes as well as Bishops of Rome. The State of the Vatican City (also known as the Holy See) was formed on February 11, 1929, with the signing of the Lateran Treaty between Italy and the Holy See. This consisted of three agreements: a treaty that recognized the autonomy of the Holy See and created the state of Vatican City; a resolution that defined relations between the government and the Church within Italy; and a financial settlement that provided the Holy See with compensation for its losses in 1870 when Victor Emmanuel II seized the Papal States and captured Rome, thus ending the temporal power of the papacy. In 1984 a revision was signed that ended certain privileges enjoyed by the Catholic Church within Italy.

Today Vatican City is the smallest independent country in the world consisting of only 109 acres (44ha) and with a population of just 911 people as of 2003. However, it employs 3,000 workers who live outside Vatican City. Financially, the country's income is derived from its worldwide banking and financial institutions, as well as Peter's Pence (voluntary contributions from Catholics worldwide), the sale of tourist memorabilia, postage stamps, admission fees to the Vatican museums, and sales of books and other publications. As well as having its own post office, Vatican City has a radio station, television broadcasting station, publishing house, electricity-generating plant, railway station, and heliport. The country also issues its own currency and passports.

The Pope is the supreme head of state and as such holds full legislative, judicial, and executive powers. His chief advisers are the College of Cardinals, who elect the Pope's successor on his death. The legal system is based on ecclesiastical law, but should this not be applicable in a particular case then the laws of the city of Rome apply. Vatican City holds full recognition under international law and can enter into international agreements. However, it is only the Holy See—in effect the government of the Roman Catholic Church—that can send or receive diplomatic representatives and in this capacity it has formal diplomatic relations with 173 nations. In 1954, the La Haye Convention recognized Vatican City as an international treasure to be respected and protected, and in 1984 it was recognized as a UNESCO world heritage site.

The colorful Swiss Guard provides security services and is responsible for public order, along with the Gendarmerie of the State of Vatican City. External security is handled by the Inspectorate of Public Security to the Vatican.

The Vatican's world-famous library and museums house collections of staggering size and value; the library alone is thought to hold an estimated 65,000 manuscripts, many in Greek and Latin, as well as more than 350,000 printed volumes. Equally renowned are the Secret Vatican Archives, containing material to which scholars did not have access until recently, although permits can now be obtained for papers written before 1922. Documents such as King Henry VIII of England's request for an annulment of his marriage to Catherine of Aragon can be found among the 30 miles (48.3km) of shelving, carefully stored within the airtight vaults where, in *Angels & Demons*, Robert Langdon conducted his desperate hunt for clues.

In 2002, Pope John Paul II announced that material from 1922–39 relating to the Vatican's relations with Germany would be made accessible, in part to counter accusations that the Church did not try to help the Jews of Europe as the Second World War approached.

In notes to visitors to the Secret Vatican Archives, Rule 14 states that it is forbidden to remove any material from the study room. Robert Langdon finds himself in a position where he must ignore this order, and takes away a priceless Galileo folio.

See also: Bernini, Gian Lorenzo; Galileo Galilei; St Peter's Basilica; Swiss Guard.

West Ponente

Bernini's *West Ponente* is the elliptical relief set into the pavement blocks in St Peter's Square in Rome, depicting the West Wind, or *Respiro di Dio* ("Breath of God"). Bernini portrays the wind in the form of a breath of air blown by an angel, which is moving away from the heart of the Vatican. The bas-relief provides a link with the element of air in the novel.

St Peter's Square is a huge public space into which tens of thousands of visitors and pilgrims converge to hear papal audiences. It is a familiar sight on television screens worldwide to witness the Pope on the balcony of St Peter's Basilica at Easter and Christmas giving his traditional *Urbi et Orbi* ("To the city [Rome] and the world") speech to the crowds below.

Despite its name, the area is not square-shaped, but rather an elliptical space more than 650 feet (198m) wide on the longer axis. Dominating the square is the Vatican obelisk that was relocated to its present position in 1586 by Pope Sixtus V. Some historians have speculated that when Bernini defined the space he enclosed an area equivalent to that of the ancient Colosseum, in an echo of Imperial Rome. The obelisk forms the centerpiece for later additions to the square, such as the two fountains added in the seventeenth century, and is surmounted by a bronze cross believed to hold a relic of the Holy Cross. A colonnade runs in four rows, symbolically forming the "motherly arms of the Church" and embracing the visitor to the square.

Although only the *West Ponente* is mentioned in the novel, all four compass points around the obelisk are marked by marble plaques, so had Dan Brown chosen the North or South Wind, tourists would be treading a different part of the pavement. Of course, in order for the design of the four locations in the novel marking the elements to form a rough cross, the West Wind is the most appropriate of the four, as it points across the city to the next clue located at Santa Maria della Vittoria, the church containing Bernini's sculpture, *The Ecstasy of St Teresa*.

See also: Bernini, Gian Lorenzo; Ecstasy of St Teresa, The; Obelisks; Santa Maria della Vittoria; St Peter's Basilica; Vatican, The.

BIBLIOGRAPHY

SCIENCE

Alfven, Hannes: *Worlds-Antiworlds: Antimatter in Cosmology* (W. H. Freeman & Co., 1966)

Battistoni, Giuseppe et al.: *Matter, Antimatter and Dark Matter* (World Scientific Publishing Company, 2002)

Camblor, Gilberto J.: *The Matter-Antimatter Cosmic Model* (Vantage Press, 2003)

Forward, Robert: *Mirror Matter: Pioneering Antimatter Physics* (Backinprint, 2001)

Harland, David M.: *The Big Bang* (Springer-Verlag, 2003)

Hawking, Stephen: *A Brief History of Time: Tenth Anniversary Edition* (Bantam, 1998)

Hawking, Stephen: *The Universe in a Nutshell* (Bantam, 2001)

Hermann, Armin et al.: *History of CERN,* Vol. I (North-Holland Press, 1987)

Lemonick, Michael D.: *Echo of the Big Bang* (Princeton University Press, 2003)

Lerner, Eric: *The Big Bang Never Happened* (Vintage, 1992)

Mitchell, William C.: *The Cult of the Big Bang: Was there a Bang?* (Cosmic Sense Books, 1995)

Schroeder, Gerald L.: *Genesis and the Big Bang Theory* (Bantam, 1992)

Silk, Joseph: *The Big Bang* (Times Books, 2000)

RELIGION

Bettenson, Henry & Maunder, Chris: *Documents of the Christian Church* (Oxford University Press, 1999)

Bokenkotter, Thomas: *A Concise History of the Catholic Church* (Doubleday, 2004)

Bruschini, Enrico: *Masterpieces of the Vatican* (Scala Publishers, 2004)

Chadwick, Henry: *The Early Church* (Penguin Books, 1993)

Cornwell, John: *A Thief in the Night: Life and Death in the Vatican* (Penguin Books, 2001)

Flannery, Austin: *Vatican Council II* (Costello Publishing Co., 1999)

Follain, John: *City of Secrets: The Truth Behind the Murders at the Vatican* (William Morrow Publishing, 2003)

Gonzalez, Justo L.: *The Story of Christianity,* Vol. I (Harper San Francisco, 1984)

Gonzalez, Justo L.: *The Changing Shape of Church History* (Chalice Press, 2002)

Hannah, John D.: *Charts of Ancient and Medieval Church History* (Zondervan Publishing Company, 2001)

Johnson, Kevin Orlin: *Why Do Catholics Do That?* (Ballantine Books, 1995)

Kertzer, David I.: *Prisoner of the Vatican: The Popes' Secret Plot to Capture Rome from the New Italian State* (Houghton Mifflin, 2004)

Kung, Hans: *The Catholic Church: A Short History* (Modern Library, 2003)

Luckert, Karl W.: *Egyptian Light and Hebrew Fire*
(State University of New York Press, 1991)

Marinelli, Luigi: *Shroud of Secrecy* (Key Porter Books, 2000)

McDowell, Bart: *Inside the Vatican* (National Geographic, 1993)

O'Connor, John et al.: *The Essential Catholic Handbook*
(Liguori Publications, 1997)

Reese, Thomas J.: *Inside the Vatican: The Politics and Organization of the Catholic Church* (Harvard University Press, 1998)

Smith, Morton: *Jesus the Magician* (Victor Gollancz, 1978)

US Catholic Church: *Catechism of the Catholic Church* (Image, 1995)

Williams, Paul L.: *The Vatican Exposed: Money, Murder and the Mafia*
(Prometheus Books, 2003)

Wilson, Jan: *Jesus: The Evidence* (HarperCollins, 1985)

Yallop, David: *In God's Name: An Investigation into the Murder of Pope John Paul I* (Bantam Dell Publishing Group, 1984)

HISTORY

Blond, Anthony: *A Scandalous History of the Roman Emperors*
(Carroll & Graf Publishers, 2000)

Boardman, John, Griffin, Jasper & Murray, Oswyn: *The Oxford Illustrated History of the Roman World* (Oxford University Press, 2001)

Claridge, Amanda, Toms, Judith & Cubberley, Tony: *Rome: An Oxford Archaeological Guide* (Oxford University Press, 1998)

Habachi, Labib: *The Obelisk of Egypt* (Dent,1978)

MacMullen, Ramsay & Lane, Eugene N.: *Paganism and Christianity, 100–425 CE: A Sourcebook* (Augsburg Fortress Press, 1992)

Matyszak, Philip: *Chronicle of the Roman Republic* (Thames & Hudson, 2003)

Maxwell-Stuart, P. G.: *Chronicle of the Popes* (Thames & Hudson, 1997)

Rubenstein, Richard E.: *When Jesus Became God: The Struggle to Define Christianity During the Last Days of Rome* (Harvest Books, 2000)

Scarre, Christopher: *The Chronicle of the Roman Emperors* (Thames & Hudson, 1995)

Scarre, Christopher: *The Penguin Historical Atlas of Ancient Rome* (Penguin, 1995)

Scullard, H. H.: *A History of the Roman World* (Routledge, 2002)

SECRET SOCIETIES

Axelrod, Alan: *The International Encyclopedia of Secret Societies and Fraternal Orders* (Facts on File, 1998)

Burkett, Larry: *The Illuminati* (WestBow Press, 1996)

Desborough, Brian: *They Cast No Shadows* (Writers Club Press, 2002)

Epperson, A. Ralph: *New World Order* (Publius Press, 1990)

Hoffman, Michael A., II: *Secret Societies and Psychological Warfare* (Independent History Press, 2001)

Howard, Michael: *The Occult Conspiracy: Secret Societies—Their Influence and Power in World History* (Destiny Books, 1989)

BIBLIOGRAPHY

Marrs, Jim: *Rule by Secrecy* (Perennial, 2001)

Monbiot, George: *Manifesto For a New World Order* (New Press, 2004)

Payson, Seth: *Proof of the Illuminati* (Invisible College Press, 2003)

Perloff, James: *Shadows of Power: The Council of Foreign Relations and the American Decline* (Western Islands Press, 1988)

Picknett, Lynn & Prince, Clive: *The Templar Revelation* (Touchstone, 1998)

Pilger, John: *The New Rulers of the World* (Verso, 2003)

Rivera, David Allen: *Final Warning: A History of the New World Order* (Conspiracy Incorporated Press, 2004)

Ross Sr, Robert Gaylon: *Who's Who of the Elite: Members of Bilderbergs, Council on Foreign Relations, & Trilateral Commission* (R. E. I. Publishers, 1996)

Sora, Steven: *Secret Societies of America's Elite: From the Knights Templar to the Skull and Bones* (Destiny Books, 2003)

Still, William T.: *New World Order: The Ancient Plan of Secret Societies* (Huntingdon House Publishers, 1990)

Sutton, Anthony C.: *America's Secret Establishment: An Introduction to the Order of Skull & Bones* (Trine Day, 2003)

Thorn, Victor: *The New World Order Exposed* (Sisyphus Press, 2003)

Tulbure, Solomon: *The Illuminati Manifesto* (Writers Club Press, 2001)

ACKNOWLEDGMENTS

This book has been a joy to work on. The roll call of honor for those directly involved goes thus:

First and foremost, my gratitude, respect, and never-ending awe goes to Susan Davies, whose efforts above and beyond the call of duty never cease to amaze me. Brilliant and beautiful is a heady mix.

Jacqueline Harvey, you are undoubtedly one of the best researchers I have ever met, second to none at sniffing out facts and snippets no one else can. Thank you.

For being a great designer, artist, and above all friend, Mark Foster earns my respect and affection in equal measure. Another great job, effortlessly done.

A brilliant writer and researcher, Mark Oxbrow also earns a gold star for timing, style, and content. Cheers, matey! Keep St Catherine safe.

Lindsay Davies at Michael O'Mara Books is a firm but fair taskmaster with a great eye for the subject matter, a rarity among editors these days. Thanks for the commission and the kind words when needed.

Robert Kirby at PFD is still a patient and understanding literary agent, for whose guidance and commitment I am forever grateful. Lamb kofte all round! I am also indebted to Catherine Cameron at PFD, to whom I give my sincere thanks.

I am similarly thankful to Simon Trewin at PFD, whose original suggestion has led to two books.

Ed and Kay Davies of Ancient World Research for Popes, Romans, and a daughter.

Geof Petch (with one "F") in the US for the DVD opportunity and the steadfast outlook in the face of much adversity.

A special thanks to Dan Brown himself, for some wonderful books.

Encouragement, support, and help were also offered in equal measure by: Gemma Smith—and Sam; Mum and

Dad (enjoy Malta); Mark and Claire Cox; Andy Gough at Kana; Greg Taylor and all at The Daily Grail website; Helen Cumberbatch and Veronica Leek at Michael O'Mara Books; Charles Symons; Rob Dimery; Caroline Davies— one of the truly great photographers; Stephen Holmes (Lost Leo here we come!); Grisha Alasadi for the great DVD edit; Alison and Neil Roberts; Robb Hoff and William Fix—let the story of Sokar be told; David Harvey; Robert Brydon in Edinburgh for the amazing conversations and hospitality; Pamela Macleod in San Francisco; Bob and Shirley Hicks in Atlanta; Jason Melton (what book?); Robert and Olivia Temple; Alan Alford; Jan and Mark Bunch for the hospitality; Salah Tawfik and family in Cairo; and Magdy Radwan, the greatest taxi driver on the planet.

PICTURE CREDITS

All photos © Simon Cox, except Raphael, the Pantheon and Galileo which are © Powerstock, and *The Ecstasy of St Teresa* which is © Gianni Dagli Orti / CORBIS.

All photo manipulation by Mark Foster (www.artifice-design.co.uk).